Bread Not Stone

Bread Not Stone

The Challenge of Feminist Biblical Interpretation

Elisabeth Schüssler Fiorenza

BEACON PRESS   BOSTON

"Women-Church: The Hermeneutical Center of Feminist Biblical Interpretation" first appeared in *Christian Feminism*, Judith L. Weidman, ed., Harper & Row, 1984. "For the Sake of Our Salvation" first appeared in *Sin, Salvation, and the Spirit*, Daniel Durken, ed., The Liturgical Press, 1979, under the title "For the Sake of Our Salvation: Biblical Interpretation as Theological Task." "The Function of Scripture in the Liberation Struggle: A Critical Feminist Hermeneutics and Liberation Theology" first appeared in *The Challenge of Liberation Theology*, L. Dale Richesin and Brian Mahan, eds., Orbis Books, 1981, under the title "Toward a Feminist Biblical Hermeneutics: Biblical Interpretation and Liberation Theology." "Discipleship and Patriarchy: Toward a Feminist Evaluation Hermeneutics" was first given as a talk for the Society of Christian Ethics. "Remembering the Past in Creating the Future: Historical-Critical Scholarship and Feminist Biblical Interpretation" is from *Feminist Perspectives on Biblical Scholarship*, Adela Yarbro Collins, ed., Scholars Press, 1985. "Toward a Critical-Theological Self-Understanding of Biblical Scholarship" first appeared in *Modern Biblical Scholarship: Its Impact on Theology and Proclamation*, Francis A. Eigo, ed., in the Villanova Monograph Series, Proceedings of the Theology Institute of Villanova University, 1984.

Beacon Press books are published under the auspices
of the Unitarian Universalist Association of
Congregations in North America,
25 Beacon Street, Boston, Massachusetts 02108
Published simultaneously in Canada by
Fitzhenry and Whiteside Limited, Toronto

Printed in the United States of America

9 8 7 6 5

Library of Congress Cataloging in Publication Data

Fiorenza, Elisabeth Schüssler, 1938–
    Bread not stone.

    Includes index.
    1. Bible—Criticism, interpretation, etc.
2. Feminism—Religious aspects—Christianity. I. Title.
BS511.2.F56 1985   220.6'01   84-14669
ISBN 0-8070-1100-2 (cloth)
ISBN 0-8070-1103-7 (paperback)

For
Feminist Poets, Ministers, Theologians
Sisters in the Struggle
Inspiring Friends

You have set sail on another ocean
without star or compass
going where the argument leads
shattering the certainties
of centuries

Janet Kalven

Contents

Introduction
Bread Not Stone

> *Who of you if their children ask for bread*
> *would give them a stone? (Matthew 7:9)*
>
> *. . . It is like leaven*
> *which a women took and hid*
> *in three measures of meal*
> *till it was all leavened. (Luke 13:21)*
>
> *Bakerwoman God*
> *Strong, brown Bakerwoman God . . .*
> *Bread well kneaded*
> *by some divine and knotty*
> *pair of knuckles,*
> *by your warm earth hands . . .*[1]

IN AN ESSAY entitled "Notes Toward Finding the Right Question" the Jewish writer Cynthia Ozick asks whether in the present discussion on "the relation of women to the Jewish Way" the right question to ask is "theological." She argues that the status of the Jewish woman is not "theological" but sociological. To change women's status in Judaism does not require changing "one iota of the status of Jewish belief."[2] Only at the end of the essay does her doubt appear in the question "What if?":

So the question arises: if, in the most fundamental text and texture of Torah, the lesser status of women is not worthy of a great "Thou shalt not," . . . then perhaps there is no essential injustice, then perhaps the common status of women is not only sanctioned, but in fact divinely ordained?[3]

In responding to Ozick's essay, the Jewish feminist theologian Judith Plaskow argues that the "right question" is indeed theological in the strictest sense of the word. The issues raised by Jewish feminism reach beyond halakha. They demand a new understanding of the Torah, God, and Israel. They ask for the acknowledgment of the "profound injustice of Torah itself," for the reception of female God-language and symbols, and finally for a new understanding of the community of Israel that would allow women to name their own religious experiences and to articulate their own theological interpretations.[4]

The essays in this book center around the same feminist theological questions and challenges that confront not only Judaism but also Christianity. I have focused on problems concerned with the Bible and biblical interpretation in church and academy. In this way I seek to develop a feminist biblical hermeneutics, that is, a theory, method, or perspective for understanding and interpretation. In doing so I also seek to contribute to the feminist articulation of a new scholarly paradigm of biblical interpretation and theology. Feminist theology begins with the experiences of women, of women-church. In our struggle for self-identity, survival, and liberation in a patriarchal society and church, Christian women have found that the Bible has been used as a weapon against us but at the same time it has been a resource for courage, hope, and commitment in this struggle. Therefore, it cannot be the task of feminist interpretation to defend the Bible against its feminist critics but to understand and interpret it in such a way that its oppressive and liberating power is clearly recognized.

A feminist hermeneutics cannot trust or accept Bible and tradition simply as divine revelation. Rather it must critically evaluate them as patriarchal articulations, since even in the last century Sarah Grimké, Matilda Joslyn Gage, and Elizabeth Cady Stanton had recognized that biblical texts are not the words of God but the words of *men.*[5] This insight particularizes the results of historical-critical scholarship that the Bible is written by human authors or male authors. This critical insight of a feminist hermeneutics has ramifications not only for historical scholarship but also for our contemporary-political situation because the Bible still functions today as a religious justification and ideological legitimization of patriarchy. To speak of power is to speak of political realities and struggles although we might not be conscious of this when we speak of the power of the Word. The Bible is not simply a religious but also a profoundly political book as it continues to inform the self-understandings of American and European "secularized" societies and cultures. Feminist biblical interpretations therefore have a critical political significance not only for women in biblical religion but for all women in Western societies.

The Bible is not only written in the words of men but also serves to legitimate patriarchal power and oppression insofar as it "renders God"[6] male and determines ultimate reality in male terms, which make women invisible or marginal. The interconnection between androcentric language and patriarchal power becomes apparent when we remember that in 1850 an act of Parliament was required to prohibit the common use of *they* for sex-indeterminable references and to legally insist that *he* stood for *she.*[7] At a time when patriarchal oppression is on the rise again in American society and religion, the development of a feminist biblical hermeneutics is not only a theological but also a profoundly political task.

The controversies that have surrounded a feminist interpretation ever since Elizabeth Cady Stanton planned and edited *The Woman's Bible* indicate that such a feminist challenge goes to the roots of religious patriarchal legitimization.[8] The recent, often violent, and seemingly irrational reactions to the *Inclusive Language Lectionary* amply prove this critical political impact of feminist biblical interpretation.[9] Writing in the *Washington Post* James J. Kilpatrick makes his point succinctly:

It is probably a waste of time, energy, and indignation

to denounce the latest efforts to *castrate* the Holy
Bible, but vandalism of this magnitude ought not to go
unremarked [emphasis added].[10]

If language determines the limits of our world, then
sacred androcentric, that is, grammatically masculine,
language symbolizes and determines our perception of
ultimate human and divine reality. Those who protest an
inclusive language translation as the "castration" of Scripture consciously or not maintain that such ultimate reality
and authority are in the words of Mary Daly "phallo-
centric."

From its inception feminist interpretation of Scripture
has been generated by the fact that the Bible was used to
halt the emancipation of slaves and women.[11] Not only
in the last century but also today patriarchal right-wing
forces in society lace their attacks against women's rights
and freedoms in the political, economic, reproductive,
intellectual, and religious arenas with biblical quotations
and appeals to scriptural authority.[12] In countless pulpits
and fundamentalist TV programs, such patriarchal attacks
are proclaimed as the Word of God while the feminist
struggle for women's liberation is denounced as "godless
humanism" that undermines the "American family." Yet
the political right does not simply misquote or misuse the
Bible as a Christian feminist apologetics seeks to argue.[13] It
can utilize certain Scriptural texts because they *are* patriarchal in their original function and intention.

Feminist interpretation therefore begins with a hermeneutics of suspicion that applies to both contemporary
androcentric interpretations of the Bible and the biblical
texts themselves. Certain texts of the Bible can be used in
the argument against women's struggle for liberation not
only because they are patriarchally misinterpreted but because they are patriarchal texts and therefore can serve to
legitimate women's subordinate role and secondary status
in patriarchal society and church. While some of us have
maintained that feminists must abandon the Bible and biblical religion, in these essays I seek to argue why feminists
cannot afford to do so. We have to reclaim biblical religion

as our own heritage because "our heritage is our power."[14] At the same time I insist that such a reclaiming of our heritage can only take place through a critical process of feminist assessment and evaluation.

Reclaiming the Bible as a feminist heritage and resource is only possible because it has not functioned only to legitimate the oppression of *all* women: freeborn, slave, black and white, native American, European and Asian, immigrant, poor, working-class and middle-class, Third World and First World women. It has also provided authorization and legitimization for women who have rejected slavery, racism, anti-Semitism, colonial exploitation, and misogynism as unbiblical and against God's will. The Bible has inspired and continues to inspire countless women to speak out and to struggle against injustice, exploitation, and stereotyping. The biblical vision of freedom and wholeness still energizes women in all walks of life to struggle against poverty, unfreedom, and denigration. It empowers us to survive with dignity and to continue the struggle when there seems to be no hope for success.[15]

A critical feminist hermeneutics of liberation therefore seeks to develop a critical dialectical mode of biblical interpretation that can do justice to women's experiences of the Bible as a thoroughly patriarchal book written in androcentric language as well as to women's experience of the Bible as a source of empowerment and vision in our struggles for liberation. Such a hermeneutics has to subject biblical texts to a dialectical process of critical readings and feminist evaluations. In order to do so it insists that *the* litmus test for invoking Scripture as the Word of God must be whether or not biblical texts and traditions seek to end relations of domination and exploitation.

In short, if we claim that oppressive patriarchal texts are the Word of God then we proclaim God as a God of oppression and dehumanization. The question is indeed "theological" in the strictest sense of the word, requiring not only a new naming of God but also a new naming of church and its use of Scripture. Such a process of naming transforms our metaphor of Scripture as "tablets of stone" on which the unchanging word of God is engraved for all times into the image of bread that nurtures, sustains, and energizes women as people of God in our struggles against injustice and oppression.

II

The hermeneutical center of such a feminist biblical interpretation—I therefore argue here—is the *ekklesia gynaikon* or women-church, the movement of self-identified women and women-identified men in biblical religion. When as a Christian I use the expression *women-church*, I do not use it as an exclusionary but as a political-oppositional term to patriarchy. It thus becomes necessary to clarify here in what way I use the term *patriarchy* as a heuristic category. I do not use the concept in the loose sense of "all men dominating all women equally," but in the classical Aristotelian sense. *Patriarchy* as a male pyramid of graded subordinations and exploitations specifies women's oppression in terms of the class, race, country, or religion of the men to whom we "belong." This definition of patriarchy enables us to use it as a basic heuristic concept for feminist analysis, one that allows us to conceptualize not only sexism but also racism, property-class relationships, and all other forms of exploitation or dehumanization as basic structures of women's oppression.

Although public life and political self-determination were restricted in Athenian democracy to the freeborn propertied male heads of patriarchal households and reserved in the patriarchal church for ordained males, I understand women-church as the dialogical community of equals in which critical judgment takes place and public freedom becomes tangible. Women-church seeks to realize the fullest meaning of the Greek New Testament notion of *ekklesia* as the public assembly of free citizens who gather in order to determine their own and their children's communal, political, and spiritual well-being. The synagogue or church of women is the gathering of all those women and men who empowered by the Holy Spirit and inspired by the biblical vision of justice, freedom, and salvation continue against all odds the struggle for liberation from patriarchal oppression in society and religion. As such the feminist movement in biblical religion is not just a civil rights but also a liberation movement. Its goal is not simply the "full humanity" of women, since humanity as we know it is male-defined. The goal is women's (religious) self-affirmation, power, and liberation from all patriarchal alienation, marginalization, and exploitation. Therefore, like other liberation theologies, feminist theology explicitly takes an advocacy position. But it articulates this advocacy position differently for women and for men. Whereas in a feminist conversion *men* must take the option for the oppressed and become women-identified, in such a conversion *women* must seek to overcome our deepest self-alienation. Since all women are socialized to respect and to identify with men, our position of advocacy must be articulated not as an "option for the oppressed" but as self-respect and self-identification *as women* in a patriarchal society and religion.

While feminist theology advocates for men a "theology of relinquishment,"[16] it articulates for women a theology of "self-affirmation." The more we identify as women and in a feminist process of conversion overcome our patriarchal self-alienation, the more we will realize that our alienation from other women—the separation between white and black women, middle-class and poor women, native American and European women, Jewish and Christian women, Protestant and Catholic women, nun-women or clergy-women and laywomen, lesbian and heterosexual women, First World and Third World women—is in the words of Adrienne Rich "a separation from ourselves."[17]

The patriarchal dehumanization and victimization of the "poorest and most despised women on earth" exhibits the full death-dealing power of patriarchy, while their struggles for liberation and their courage to survive is the fullest experience of God's grace in our midst. The *locus* of divine revelation and grace is therefore not simply the Bible or the tradition of a patriarchal church but the "church of women" in the past and in the present. God's nurturing presence "reveals" its power in the struggles of all women who seek to live "the option for our women selves" in a patriarchal society and religion. Conversely, the "option for our women selves" is the "option for the most oppressed women" and the commitment to their struggles.

Such an option allows us "to find God in ourselves" and "to love Her fiercely, to love Her fiercely."[18]

The spiritual authority of women-church rests on the experience of God's sustaining grace and liberating presence in the midst of our struggles for justice, freedom, and wholeness of all. It rests not simply on the "experience of women" but on the experience of women struggling for liberation from patriarchal oppression:

> The dream of freedom for oneself in a world in which all women are free emerges from one's life experience in which one is not free, precisely because one is a woman. The liberation of women is thus not an abstract goal . . . but is the motive for that process. Individual freedom and the freedom of all women are linked when one has reached the critical consciousness that we are united first in our unfreedom.[19]

A feminist critical theology of liberation, therefore, must reject all religious texts and traditions that contribute to "our unfreedom." In a public feminist critical discourse this theology seeks to evaluate *all* biblical texts, interpretations, and contemporary uses of the Bible for their contribution to the religious legitimization of patriarchy as well as for their stand toward patriarchal oppression. A feminist critical theology of liberation therefore develops a hermeneutics of critical evaluation rather than one of correlation.[20]

What leads us to perceive biblical texts as oppressive or as providing resources in the struggle for liberation from patriarchal oppression or as models for the transformation of the patriarchal church into women-church is not a revealed principle or a special canon of texts that can claim divine authority. Rather it is the experience of women struggling for liberation and wholeness. Insofar as biblical texts remember the struggles of our foremothers and forefathers against patriarchal oppression and their experience of God's sustaining presence, they can become paradigmatic for women-church and "inspire" our own struggles and visions of life.

I have therefore proposed that we understand the Bible as a structuring prototype of women-church rather than as a timeless archetype , as an open-ended paradigm that sets experience in motion and structures transformations. Rather than reducing the biblical multiformity and richness of experience to abstract principles or impulses to be applied to new situations, I suggest the notion of a historical prototype open to its own critical transformation. This notion of the Bible as a formative root-model of women-church allows us to explore models and traditions of emancipatory praxis as well as of patriarchal oppression. It allows us to reclaim the whole Bible, not as a normative immutable archetype, but as an experiential authority that can "render God" although it is written in the "language of men." It allows us to reclaim the Bible as enabling resource, as bread not stone, as legacy and heritage, not only of patriarchal religion but also of women-church as the discipleship of equals. The perception of the Bible as a historical prototype provides women-church with a sense of its ongoing history as well as its Christian identity.

In short, through a process of critical evaluation as well as structural and creative transformation the Bible can become Holy Scripture for women-church. Insofar as the interpretive model proposed here does not identify biblical revelation with androcentric texts and patriarchal structures, it maintains that such revelation is found among the discipleship community of equals in the present and in the past.[21] Since the model proposed here locates revelation, not in androcentric texts, but in the experience of God's grace and presence among women struggling for liberation from patriarchal oppression and dehumanization, this model requires a feminist critical hermeneutics of the Bible in the context of women-church.[22]

III

A feminist reading of the Bible requires both a transformation of our patriarchal understandings of God, Scripture, and the Church and a transformation in the self-understanding of historical-critical scholarship and the theological disciplines.

Such an attempt encounters resistance from two groups. Women often consider theoretical and methodological discussions as a male "trip," as a flight from practical engagement and political activism. While this certainly can be the case, I would nevertheless argue that feminists cannot afford to be anti-intellectual. Since "knowledge is power," women have to become involved in the production and distribution of knowledge. Women's systemic exclusion from scholarship and intellectual influence is an important aspect of our powerlessness. This is especially true in theology, since women only recently gained access to the academic disciplines of theology. Even theologically trained women are more hesitant to enter a critical theological discussion than to share their religious experiences and spiritual insights.

I have therefore begun to use technical theological terms such as *hermeneutics* in order to elaborate in lectures and workshops the concept of theology-anxiety by analogy with the notion of math-anxiety, into which women are systematically socialized.[23] The following two reactions, which I recently received after a lecture on feminist hermeneutics before an audience of ministers and theology students, will illustrate my point. First, although I had spoken about theology anxiety, explaining how the "power of theological naming" was stolen from us, one of the few male participants complimented me on my rigorous, intellectual approach but counseled that I should not use difficult theological terms such as *hermeneutics* because "women do not have the sophistication to understand them." Later, a women participant related that in her senior year in college she wrote a paper for a seminar on the Old Testament in which she used the word *hermeneutics.* To her surprise the professor had circled the word in red ink and written in the margin; "What a fancy word! Please use simpler terms." After listening to my elaborations on how women are kept from theological thinking, she understood for the first time why she had been censured, although the literature she had consulted had used the term frequently.

The second group that finds it difficult to accept that feminist studies in general and feminist theology in particular seek to effect a paradigm shift in the academic disciplines comprises established members of the academy. Feminist theology is often tolerated as a "woman's affair" or as supplementary to male scholarship, but not as a different perspective and method for doing theology. Women in the academy are seen as "competent" scholars when we adopt the investigative methods and theoretical frameworks of our male mentors. Women scholars are expected to gather "data," to faithfully apply standard methods, or to do routine research in insignificant areas, but not to cut new paths, to establish new theoretical frameworks, or to write groundbreaking works, works that will change the discipline. The feminist sociologist Dorothy Smith describes this experience:

> The universe of ideas, images and themes—the symbolic modes which are the general currency of thought— have been either produced by men or controlled by them. Insofar as women's work and experience has been entered into it, it has been on terms decided by men and because it has been approved by men.[21]

In her book *Women and Ideas and What Men Have Done to Them* the Australian feminist scholar Dale Spender seeks to recover the lost intellectual history of women from Aphra Behn to Adrienne Rich. She argues that the invisibility of women, the absence of women's intellectual voice, the experience that every feminist work has been received as if it emerged from nowhere, is fundamental to the perpetuation of patriarchal power. Women thinkers and artists disappear from the historical consciousness not only of men but also of women, because patriarchy demands that any articulation of the central problem of male power that confronts women should remain invisible and unreal.

As this book demonstrates for centuries women have been challenging men, and men have used punitive measures against them; for centuries women have been claiming that the world and men look very different from the perspective of women. Far from being an unusual claim, it is a common assertion of women of the past and a familiar issue in contemporary feminism that women's meanings and values have been excluded from what have been put forward as society's meanings and values.[25]

Needless to say, women-church's values and visions have also been excluded from the church's or God's values and words. Feminist theology seeks to interrupt this theological and spiritual patriarchal silencing of women. It listens carefully to women's spiritual and religious experiences in order to define new theoretical frameworks and approaches that would allow us to bring women's patriarchal silences "into speech,"[26] and to make our values, insights, and visions integral to the theological discourse of the church.

The essays in this volume seek to develop a critical feminist hermeneutics and to work out the ramifications for different areas of theological inquiry. The first chapter attempts to delineate a comprehensive multidimensional model of a critical feminist hermeneutics. Chapters 2, 3, and 4 address issues and problems of the historical-critical interpretation of the Bible raised by pastoral theology, liberation theology, and moral theology or ethics. Chapters 5 and 6 examine methodological and hermeneutical discussions in historical and literary critical scholarship of the Bible in order to illustrate that a feminist critical hermeneutics of liberation can contribute to the transformation of the discipline.

A comprehensive introduction to the issues discussed in a feminist critical hermeneutics of Scripture is given in the first chapter. Here I propose that feminist theology distinguish between a hermeneutics of suspicion, a hermeneutics of proclamation, a hermeneutics of remembrance and historical reconstruction as well as a hermeneutics of ritualization and celebration. These four elements of a multidimensional feminist model of interpretation are rooted in the experience and praxis of women-church. They were crystallized in response to the discussions of my work in the AAR feminist liberation theology section of the American Academy of Religion, which was coordinated and chaired by Letty Russell.[27] Our diverse questions and methodological or theological differences helped me to clarify my own approach while at the same time recognizing our common concerns.

In the second chapter I address the tensions between historical-critical scholarship and the use of the Bible in the church. I relate this discussion to the history of biblical interpreation and argue that all members of the Church need to become subjects of biblical interpretation. Biblical interpretation should no longer be restricted to ecclesiastics, historians of religions, or preachers, because the Bible is entrusted to all of us for the "sake of our salvation."

I attempt to chart in the third chapter the commonalities and differences in experience and method that exist between the hermeneutical proposals of liberation theologians and feminist theologians. Liberation theologians emphasize that the God of the Bible is on the side of the oppressed and impoverished, and they are able to cite many biblical texts in support of this contention. Feminist theologians do not find an explicit feminist-critical principle or tradition in the Bible. Instead we are faced with the fact that the Bible is written in male language, which mirrors and perpetuates patriarchal culture and religion.

The fourth chapter is a concrete example of a feminist critical interpretation. In elaborating the tensions between the early Christian ethos and its patriarchal social world, I seek to show that the so-called household-codes of the New Testament are patriarchal texts that must be critically evaluated rather than justified as scholarly interpretations or some feminist apologetics are prone to do. Therefore, a critical feminist hermeneutics challenges biblical scholarship as well as Christian ethics to develop a critical evaluative hermeneutics that can elaborate the oppressive political impact of the Bible because such a hermeneutics acknowledges that concrete demands for justice have primacy in the logic of Christian theological discourse.[28]

Chapters 5 and 6 address the self-understanding of contemporary biblical scholarship. They seek to show why an objectivist-reified self-understanding of biblical scholarship is not sufficiently aware of the hermeneutical insights of contemporary historiography and thus is not able to fulfill its critical-historical task. The basic thesis of these chapters is that the tensions between so-called objectivist, value-neutral, scientific, historical biblical scholarship and a committed feminist biblical scholarship are not the result of the theoretical deficiencies of feminist scholarship. Liberation and feminist theologies challenge, therefore, historical-literary biblical scholarship to abandon the posture of scientific facticity, value-neutrality, and antiquarian mentality and to recover historical consciousness as remembrance for the present and the future.

Since all the chapters approach the same problem from different angles, they necessarily overlap at points. Nevertheless they represent a coherent and consistent argument for a feminist critical hermeneutics that can not only introduce students to the problems of biblical interpretation but also further scholarly discussion. Restating the same insights and arguments in different contexts will enable readers who are not conversant with biblical and hermeneutical problems to become more familiar with the theological idiom and in the process of reading to exorcise their theology-anxiety.

A comparison with a recent philosophical work on the present intellectual discourse on hermeneutics might help to situate the discussions and proposals of this book. In *Beyond Objectivism and Relativism: Science, Hermeneutics, and Praxis*, Richard Bernstein points out that in contrast with European scholars, Anglo-American thinkers have become interested in hermeneutics only during the past decade or so. Analyzing the contributions of Gadamer, Habermas, Kuhn, Rorty, and Arendt to the "new conversation" about human rationality, he develops a complex argument that challenges the dichotomy between objectivism and relativism.

Rather than seeking ultimate foundations and a "fixed Archimedean point" on which to secure our thoughts, beliefs, and actions, these thinkers attempt to overcome the either/or of objectivism and relativism in a practical-moral concern for ways in which we can foster a "reawakening consciousness of solidarity." Bernstein points out that we encounter in their arguments something like a circle that can be compared to the hermeneutical circle. Dialogical communities that can foster solidarity, freedom, and public discourse presuppose incipient forms of such communal life.

> There is no guarantee . . . no "logic of history" that must inevitably lead to dialogical communities that embrace all of humanity in which reciprocal judgment, practical discourse, and rational persuasion flourish. If anything we should have learned how much the contemporary world conspires against it and undermines it.

Bernstein therefore concludes that it is not

> sufficient to come up with some new variations of arguments that will show, once and for all, what is wrong with objectivism and relativism, or even open up a way of thinking that can move us beyond objectivism and relativism; such a movement gains "reality and power" only if we dedicate ourselves to the practical task of furthering the type of solidarity, participation, and mutual recognition that is founded in dialogical communities.[29]

A comparison with Bernstein's proposal underlines three important contributions that the critical feminist hermeneutics developed in these essays can make to the general discussion of biblical hermeneutics. The chapters in this book diagnose that biblical interpretation and theology are caught in the same Cartesian anxiety and either/or of objectivism and relativism. I have argued therefore that rather than seek a "revealed" Archimedean point in the shifting sand of biblical-historical relativity—be it a liberating tradition, text, or principle in the Bible—a feminist critical hermeneutics has to explore and assess whether and how Scripture can become an enabling, motivating resource and empowering authority in women's struggle for justice, liberation, and solidarity.[30]

Moreover, Bernstein recognizes that much of humanity has been and still is systematically excluded from participating in such dialogical communities. But he does not develop this insight as a critical impulse for practical discourse. By making women the subjects of biblical interpretation and critical theological evaluation, a feminist critical hermeneutics takes the experience of women's exclusion and invisibility as its critical point of departure. Finally, whereas such dialogical communities remain for Bernstein a *telos* that he cannot name concretely and identify historically, I have put forward women-church as the dialogical community that is incipiently given but still needs to be realized in feminist conversion and historical struggle for liberation from patriarchal oppression.

Although a critical feminist hermeneutics must seek to transform the discipline of biblical scholarship and theology, its primary commitment is not to the academy but to women-church and to all women struggling for dignity, self-affirmation, survival, and freedom in cultural and societal patriarchy. Its primary questions and problems are not those of the academy but those of women-church. Its validity and impact will depend on how much it is able to reclaim the Bible as a resource for women-church. In order to do our work feminist scholars and students of the Bible must therefore heed the warning of the feminist poet and social activist Renny Golden in "Academic Women":

Rainbow fish precious, picked from the catch.
You swim through their corridors, upstream.
You've done their task and ours,
double labor familiar as laundry.
We quote from your books,
claim you before men
who tell our bodies they're all we got.
Sisters, light dazzles when it's pure.
Beacons: remember you illumine someone's way.
Their seduction is naming you stars . . .
brilliant, singular, without purpose.

When you speak of the common woman, the poor woman
get the accent right.
Consider the net enfolding you.
Outside we are thousands.
Unless you swim in our waters,

you'll miss depth.
From time to time you will have to mention us,
but you won't get it right.[31]

1.

Women-Church
*The Hermeneutical Center of Feminist
Biblical Interpretation*

THE SECOND LETTER of John—the only writing of the
New Testament addressed to a woman—was written "for
the sake of the truth that dwells among us and will be with
us forever." Biblical interpretation as theological interpretation is concerned with the divine presence dwelling
among the people of God in the past and present. Feminist
biblical interpretation makes explicit that divine truth and
revelatory presence are found among women, who are the
invisible members of the people of God. It makes explicit
that the receivers and proclaimers of revelation are not
solely men but also women. It thus seeks to interrupt the
theological silence and ecclesial invisibility of women so
that God's grace and truth may be revealed among us in
their fullness.

The critical rereading of the Bible in a feminist key and
from women's perspectives is in the process of uncovering
lost traditions and correcting mistranslations, of peeling
away layers of androcentric scholarship and rediscovering
new dimensions of biblical symbols and theological meanings. In Bible study groups, sermons, and seminars, women
rediscover our biblical heritage and realize that this heritage is part of our power today. The rediscovery on a
popular and academic level is made possible by two basic
shifts, in our perception of the world and reality and in
our perception of the function of biblical texts and interpretations. Such paradigm shifts are on the one hand a
shift from an androcentric to a feminist perception of the
world and on the other hand a shift from an apologetic

focus on biblical authority to a feminist articulation of
contemporary women's experience and struggle against
patriarchal oppression in biblical religion.

I. From an Androcentric to a Feminist
Interpretive Framework

The resurgence of the women's movement in the 1960s
not only revived women's political struggle for civil rights
and equal access to academic institutions but also brought
forth feminist studies as a new intellectual discipline. In all
areas of scientific and intellectual knowledge there now
exist courses and research projects that seek to expand our
knowledge of women's cultural and historical contributions as well as to challenge the silence about us in historiography, literature, sociology, and all the human sciences.
Such feminist scholarship is compensatory as well as revolutionary. It has inaugurated a scientific revolution that engenders a scholarly paradigm shift from an androcentric—
male-centered—world view and perspective to an inclusive
feminist comprehension of the world, human life, and history.

While androcentric scholarship takes *man* as the paradigmatic human being, feminist scholarship insists on the
reconceptualization of our intellectual frameworks so that
they become truly inclusive of all human experience and
articulate the male experience of truth as one particular
experience and perception of reality. Feminist scholarship
therefore throws into question our dominant cultural
mind-set, articulated in male-generic language, classical
texts, scholarly frameworks, and scientific reconstructions
that make women invisible and marginal. This mind-set
promotes the view that women's experiences and cultural
contributions are less valuable, less important, or less
significant than men's. Feminist studies challenge male
symbolic representations, androcentric language, and the
habitual consciousness of two "sex classes" as "naturally
given" facts and categories in our language and thought
world. These studies point to the interaction between
language and society, sexual stereotypes and culture,
gender and race, as social constructs and political legitimi-

zations. Sexism, racism, imperialism, and militarism constitute different aspects of the same language of oppression
in our society.

Feminist studies articulate the feminist paradigm in different ways and according to various philosophical perspectives. While liberal scholarship may seek to show that
women were and are equal to men without critically reflecting on the male-centered framework underlying such
an argument, feminists with an existentialist or a sociology
of knowledge approach use as their main heuristic category
androcentrism or phallocentrism. Whereas socialist feminists use as their key analytical category the relationship
between social class and gender, Third World feminists find
the relationship between racism, colonialism, and sexism
most significant. This variety of emphases and approaches
results in different conceptions and frameworks of feminism, of women's liberation, and of being human in
the world.

A similar diversity in approach is also found among feminists in biblical religion and feminist theologians. There
exists not one feminist theology or *the* feminist theology
but many different expressions and articulations of feminist theology. These articulations not only share in the
diverse presuppositions and perspectives of feminist studies but also function within the frameworks of divergent
theological perspectives, such as neo-orthodoxy, evangelical theology, liberal theology, liberation theology, process
theology, and various confessional theological perspectives.
As theological articulations they are rooted in the ecclesial
visions and political situations of the Christian or Jewish
communities to whom they are committed.

Yet feminist theologies introduce a radical shift into all
forms of traditional theology, for they insist that the
central commitment and accountability for feminist theologians is not to *the* church as a male institution but to
women in the churches, not to *the* tradition as such but to
a feminist transformation of Christian traditions, not to
the Bible as a whole but to the liberating Word of God
finding expression in the biblical writings. Those of us who
see our work and ourselves as part of the women's movement in the churches and define our allegiances not solely

in terms of the women's movement in society and culture tend to articulate our theology in these broader terms, that is, in relation to the religio-political goals, the spiritual needs, and the communal problems of women in biblical religion. The theological discussions on an inclusive translation of the Bible or on the question of God language occur in this context within organized biblical religion.

Those of us who do not consider ourselves members of biblical communities but are committed to the religious quest of women in different cultures and religions tend to formulate our questions and theological perspectives more in terms of a religious studies approach within the academy. In this approach the situation of women in the Bible or in early Christianity is studied as part of the Oriental or Greco-Roman world and religion to which the biblical writings belong. Such research has had significant results with respect to women in Egypt, Rome, or Judaism and has shattered the apologetic assumption that biblical religion has emancipated ancient women.The Feminist Hermeneutics group within the Liberation Theology group of the AAR is representative of the first approach, and Women in the Biblical World section of the Society of Biblical Literature is representative of the second approach.

Jewish feminists in turn have pointed out that a Jewish feminist biblical interpretation has to wrestle with a different set of theological problems and hermeneutical frameworks than has Christian feminist scholarship of the Bible. Christians not only claim the New Testament and the Hebrew Bible as their own Holy Scriptures, they also have to deal with the anti-Judaism codified in the New Testament. Moreover, Judaism has developed distinct exegetical methods and hermeneutical traditions. Finally, because theology as a concept is not as central to Jewish as to Christian thought and life, the very concept of a Jewish feminist theology becomes less important. Therefore we cannot speak about a feminist biblical interpretation as long as Jewish feminist hermeneutics has not developed in its own right and articulated its own specific questions and approaches. The following must thus clearly be understood as a feminist Christian theological perspective, and I have defined this perspective as a feminist critical theology of liberation. This articulation of my own feminist theological perspective has grown out of my experience as a Catholic Christian woman and is indebted to historical-critical scholarship, critical theory, and political as well as liberation theology.

At this point I should explicate my undestanding of feminism and of patriarchal oppression. Feminism is not just a theoretical world view or perspective but a women's liberation movement for social and ecclesiastical change. Similarly, patriarchal oppression is not identical with androcentrism or sexism. It is not just a "dualistic ideology" or androcentric world construction in language but a sociopolitical system and social structure of graded subjugations and oppressions. Although this patriarchal system has undergone significant changes throughout history, it has prevailed as the dominant sociopolitical structure of the last five thousand years or so. Its classical expression is found in Aristotelian philosophy, which has decisively influenced not only Christian theology but also Western culture and political philosphy.[1]

Patriarchy defines not just women as the "other" but also subjugated peoples and races as the "other" to be dominated. It defines women, moreover, not just as the other of men but also as subordinated to men in power insofar as it conceives of society as analogous to the patriarchal household, which was sustained by slave labor. Women of color and poor women are doubly and triply oppressed in such a patriarchal social system. A critical feminist theology of liberation, therefore, does not speak of male oppressors and female oppressed, of all men over all women, but rather of patriarchy as a pyramidal system and hierarchical structure of society and church in which women's oppression is specified not only in terms of race and class but also in terms of "marital" status. The understanding of feminist liberation as a struggle to overcome this oppression was expressed by black activist Anna Cooper in 1892:

> Let women's claim be as broad in the concrete as in the abstract. We take our stand on the solidarity of humanity, the oneness of life, and the unnaturalness and injustice of all special favoritism, whether of sex, race, country, or condition. . . . The colored woman feels that women's cause is one and universal; and that

not till the image of God whether in parian or ebony, is sacred and inviolable; not till race, color, sex, and condition are seen as accidents, and not the substance of life; not till the universal title of humanity to life, liberty, and the pursuit of happiness is conceded to be inalienable to all; not till then is woman's cause won— not the white woman's, nor the black woman's, nor the red woman's, but the cause of every man and every woman who has writhed silently under a mighty wrong. Woman's wrongs are thus indissolubly linked with all undefended woe and the acquirement of her "rights" will mean the final triumph of all right over might; the supremacy of the moral forces of reason, and justice, and love in the government of the nations of earth.[2]

A feminist theology of liberation must remain first and foremost a critical theology of liberation as long as women suffer the injustice and oppression of patriarchal structures. This theology explores the particular experiences of women struggling for liberation from systemic patriarchy and at the same time indicts all patriarchal structures and texts, especially those of biblical religion. Such a theology seeks to name theologically the alienation, anger, pain, and dehumanization engendered by patriarchal sexism and racism in society and church. At the same time it seeks to articulate an alternative vision of liberation by exploring women's experiences of survival and salvation in our struggle against patriarchal oppression and degradation, as well as by assessing Christian texts, traditions, and communities in terms of such liberation from patriarchal oppression.

Such a critical feminist theology of liberation does not advocate the co-optation of women's religious powers by ecclesiastical patriarchy or the feminist abandonment of biblical vision and community. Its feminist heuristic key is not a dual theological anthropology of masculine and feminine, or the concept of the complementarity of the sexes, or a metaphysical principle of female ascendancy. Its formulations are based on the radical assumption that gender is socially, politically, economically, and theologically con-

structed and that such a social construction serves to perpetuate the patriarchal exploitation and oppression of all
women, which is most fully expressed in the fate of the
"poorest and most despised women on earth."
A feminist critical theology of liberation seeks to enable
Christian women to explore theologically the structural sin
of patriarchal sexism, in a feminist conversion to reject its
spiritual internalizations, and to become the *ekklesia* of
women, women-church. In exorcising the internalized
structural evil of patriarchal sexism as well as in calling the
whole church to conversion and repentance, Christian feminism and feminist theology reclaim the right and power to
articulate our own theology, to reclaim our own spirituality, and to determine our own and our sisters religious life.
As the church of women we celebrate our religious powers
and ritualize our visions for change and liberation. We
bond together in struggling with all women for liberation,
and we share our strength in nurturing each other in the
full awareness and recognition that the church of women is
always the *ecclesia reformanda*, the church on the way to
and in need of conversion and "revolutionary patience,"
patience with our own failures as well as with those of our
sisters. Reconciliation is pivotal in this process of becoming "a people of God." We need to listen to each other's
experiences, to cease speaking for all women, and to overcome our sense of guilt in solidarity and support.

To advocate the women's liberation movement in biblical religion as the hermeneutical center of a feminist
critical theology of liberation and to speak of the church
of women does not mean to advocate a separatist strategy
but to underline the visibility of women in biblical religion
and to safeguard our freedom from spiritual male control.
Just as we speak of the church of the poor, of an African
or Asian church, of Presbyterian, Episcopalian, or Roman
Catholic churches, without relinquishing our theological
vision of the universal Church, so we may speak of the
church of women as a manifestation of this universal
Church. Since all Christian churches suffer from the structural evil of patriarchal sexism and racism in various
degrees, the church of women as a feminist movement of
self-identified women and women-identified men tran-

scends all traditional man-made denominational lines. The commitment and mission of women-church is defined by the solidarity with the most despised women suffering from the triple oppression of sexism, racism, and poverty. A feminist biblical interpretation that develops within the framework of a critical theology of liberation must be situated within the feminist community of women in biblical religion.

II. The Bible as the Book of Women-Church

Taking as our hermeneutical criterion the authority of women's experience struggling for liberation, we must ask whether the Bible as the product of a patriarchal culture can also be the Sacred Scripture for the church of women. This is a difficult question, since the Bible has been used to halt the emancipation of women, slaves, and colonized peoples. Elizabeth Cady Stanton has eloquently summed up this use of the Bible against women's demand for political and ecclesial equality.

> From the inauguration of the movement for woman's emancipation the Bible has been used to hold her in the "divinely ordained sphere" prescribed in the Old and New Testaments. . . . Creeds, codes, Scriptures and statutes are all based on this idea.[3]

Whenever women protest against political discrimination, economic exploitation, sexual violence, or our secondary status in biblical religion, the Bible is invoked against us. At the same time the Bible has provided theological support for Christian women and men who rejected slavery, poverty, and patriarchal sexism as against God's will.

While clergymen invoked the Bible in the last century in order to bar women from speaking in public and in this century in order to prevent the ordination of women, women have pointed to other biblical texts to legitimize their claim to public speaking and the ministry. While many feminists reject the Bible as totally oppressive and patriarchal, others have attempted to show that the Bible correctly interpreted preaches the emancipation of women. While Christian apologists argue that only feminist ignorance or misunderstanding leads to the rejection of the Bible, Christian Biblicists maintain that feminism is a perversion of God's word and a godless humanism. While Christian feminists seek a "usable past," Christian conservatives claim that women can find happiness only by living out the scriptural injunctions to submission.

In this political-religious controversy, certain passages in Scripture are used to justify one's particular interests. Central to this apologetic debate is the interest in legitimizing one's own position by reference to biblical authority. Both detractors and defenders of women's liberation refer to the Bible because of its ecclesial authority and societal influence. The focal point of this political apologetics is the Bible rather than the experience of women, for both sides seek to prove or disprove the patriarchal character of certain biblical texts.

By contrast, postbiblical feminists do not challenge only certain passages and statements of the Bible; instead they reject the Bible in its entirety, as irredeemable for feminists. Recognizing that androcentric language and patriarchal traditions have erased women from biblical texts and made us "nonbeings" in biblical history, they argue that the Bible is irretrievable for feminists who are committed to women's struggle for liberation. The Bible ignores women's experience, speaks of God in male language, and sustains women's powerlessness in society and church. It legitimizes women's social and ecclesiastical subordination and second-class status as well as male dominance and violence against women, especially against those caught in patriarchal marriage relationships. Because of its androcentric-patriarchal character, feminists must reject the authority of the Bible. Revisionist interpretations are at best a waste of time and at worst a co-optation of feminism by patriarchal biblical religion.

Christian apologists as well as postbiblical feminists not only overlook the experiences of women in biblical religion but also assume that the Bible has authority independently of the community to which it belongs. If this apologetic debate seeks to salvage or to reject the religious authority of the Bible for women today, it understands the

Bible as a mythical archetype rather than as a historical prototype open to feminist theological transformation. As mythical archetype the Bible can be either accepted or rejected, but not critically evaluated. A mythical archetype takes historically limited experiences and texts and posits them as universals, which then become authoritative and normative for all times and cultures. For instance, many scriptural texts speak of God as a male, patriarchal, all-powerful ruler. Therefore, it is argued, feminists have to accept the patriarchal male language and God of the Bible, or they have to reject the Bible and leave behind biblical religion.

By ascribing universal implications to specific historical texts and cultural situations, the mythical archetype establishes an ideal form for all times, an unchanging pattern of behavior and theological structure for the community in which it serves as Sacred Scripture. The Bible as archaic myth therefore constitutes the enduring order and perspective of biblical religion, reflecting unchangeable ontological patterns and perennial models for human behavior and communal life. Since biblical texts as the Word of God are formulated in androcentric language and are products and reflections of patriarchal cultures, they express a patriarchal system and androcentric view valid for all times.

Because the Bible is stamped by patriarchal oppression but claims to be the Word of God, it perpetuates an archetypal oppressive myth that must be rejected by feminists on the one hand and must be maintained over feminism by biblical religion on the other hand. The archetypal myth of the Bible as the Word of God has been challenged by historical-critical scholarship and has undergone significant modifications in the last centuries. Although biblical and theological scholarship is well aware of the difficulties raised by such an archetypal understanding of the Bible, ecclesiastical authority and popular preaching has not quite accepted the challenge of historical-critical scholarship to the archetypal definition of biblical inspiration.

In the dominant paradigm of biblical interpretation three hermeneutical models are interrelated but can be distinguished (see chap. 2). First, the doctrinal model of interpretation centers around the teachings and creeds of the Church and refers to the Bible in order to prove and substantiate patriarchal teachings and symbolic structures. For instance, this model includes the debate on whether Paul teaches the subordination of women or allows for the full equality of women in the church, and therefore for women's ordination. The model subscribes fully to the archetypal understanding of the Bible, especially in literal interpretations, and conceives of biblical revelation as verbal inspiration. Although evangelical feminism modifies this doctrinal model, it seeks to remain within the boundaries set by it, in order to remain faithful to biblical revelation.

The second model in biblical interpretation is the historical-factual model. It was developed in reaction to the doctrinal model and often identifies biblical truth and authority with historical or textual factualness. The Bible is understood as a collection of historical writings that are more or less true, that is, historically reliable. Nevertheless, the canonical collection of early Christian writings is not comprehensive and therefore historical-critical scholarship must study all extant early Christian writings. The truth of biblical religion resides in those traditions and texts that are historically reliable, that is, that tell us what actually happened. If for instance scholars can prove that the "empty tomb stories" in the New Testament are secondary legends of the community, then scholars cannot accord historical reliability and theological significance to the resurrection witness of Mary Magdalene and the women disciples. Or, if Jesus chose only men and not women as his followers, then he established a pattern for all times and women cannot become apostolic successors and be ordained as priests. This model thus establishes the archetypal significance of the Bible through historical verification.

The third model of biblical interpretation is the dialogical-pluralistic model of form and redaction criticism, which seeks to recover all canonical texts and traditions and to understand them as theological responses to their historical-communal situations. The Bible thus becomes a kaleidoscope mirroring and reflecting the pluralistic and multifaceted life and faith of biblical communities in their historical-cultural circumstances.

But the Bible contains not only a variety of texts but also many contradictory or even oppressive texts and symbols that cannot all have the same theological authority for communities today. Although this dialogical-pluralistic model moves away from the archetypal understanding of the Bible in its historical-critical interpretations, it resorts to the archetypal paradigm in its theological evaluations and normative claims, in its efforts to identify God's voice in the polyphony of biblical voices. Acknowledging the multiform theological character of the canon, it must establish a "canon within the canon," a theological criterion and measuring rod with which to assess the truth and authority of the various biblical texts and traditions. This "measure" is derived from the canon, that is, the collection of biblical writings acknowledged by Christians as Sacred Scriptures. This attempt to define a "canonical" criterion began with Marcion and has become especially important for the dialogical-pluralistic understanding of the Bible.

In response to the factual-historical model, the neo-orthodox "canon within the canon" debate attempts to identify theologically those texts and traditions of the Bible that can serve as a measuring rod for evaluating the claims to truth in the pluralistic collection of canonical writings. This neo-orthodox model no longer understands the whole Bible as archetypal myth but only those texts and traditions that are judged canonical, as expressing the Word of God. It identifies such a canon either along historical-factual lines (e.g., the authentic Jesus traditions, the *ipsissima verba* of Jesus, or the earliest traditions of the apostolic church), or along doctrinal lines (e.g., the gospel message, the Pauline doctrine of justification by faith, or the creed), or along philosophical lines of argument (e.g., revelatory essence and historical accidental statements, timeless truth and culturally conditioned language, universal revelation and historical expression, constant tradition and changing traditions, or the liberating impulses of the biblical vision and its oppressive patriarchal articulations).

The search for a critical principle of revelation or for a normative biblical tradition is also found in feminist theology. For instance, Rosemary Radford Ruether has developed a method of correlation and has proposed the distinction between the liberating-prophetic critique of biblical religion and its cultural deformations,[4] and L. Russell has reformulated her distinction of constant and changing traditions with reference to the eschatological future of God's liberation. "The bible has authority because it witnesses to God's liberating action on behalf of God's creation."[5] But the attempt to derive a critical universal principle or normative tradition from particular historical texts and specific cultural situations indicates that such a feminist theological hermeneutics still adheres to the archetypal biblical paradigm that establishes universal principles and normative patterns. Since it is impossible for feminist theologians to accept *all* canonical texts and traditions, we must claim that certain texts or traditions are not deformed by androcentrism or have been critical of patriarchy in order to reclaim the Bible as normative and authoritative for feminists in biblical religion.

A feminist hermeneutics must seriously take into account the androcentric character of biblical language on the one hand and the patriarchal stamp of all biblical traditions on the other hand. By distinguishing language and content, patriarchal expression and liberating tradition, androcentric text and feminist "witness," this hermeneutics seems to rely on an untenable linguistic-philosophical position that divides form and content, linguistic expression and revelatory truth. By choosing one tradition, text, or biblical dynamics it is in danger of advocating a reductionist method of theological critique and of relinquishing the historical richness of biblical experience.

A feminist critical interpretation of the Bible cannot take as its point of departure the normative authority of the biblical archetype, but must begin with women's experience in their struggle for liberation. In doing so this mode of interpretation subjects the Bible to a critical feminist scrutiny and to the theological authority of the church of women, an authority that seeks to assess the oppressive or liberating dynamics of all biblical texts. Just as Jesus according to the Gospels realized freedom toward Scripture and tradition for the sake of human well-being and wholeness of (cf. Mark 2:27), so too a feminist critical hermeneutics seeks to assess the function of the Bible in terms of women's liberation and wholeness. It follows Augustine, Thomas, and the Second Vatican Council in formulating a criterion or canon that limits inspired truth and revelation to matters pertaining to the salvation, freedom, and liberation of all, especially women.[6]

But it derives this canon, *not* from the biblical writings, but from the contemporary struggle of women against racism, sexism, and poverty as oppressive systems of patriarchy and from its systematic explorations in feminist theory. It can do so because it does not understand the Bible as archetype but as historical prototype or as a formative root-model of biblical faith and life. Its vision of liberation and salvation is informed by the biblical prototype but is not derived from it. It places biblical texts under the authority of feminist experience insofar as it maintains that revelation is ongoing and takes place "for the sake of our salvation." It does not seek identification with certain biblical texts and traditions, but rather solidarity with women in biblical religion. As the church of women, we are called not to reproduce biblical structures and traditions but to remember and transform our biblical heritage.

Understanding the Bible as a historical prototype rather than as a mythical archetype allows the church of women to make connections with our own experiences, historical struggles, and feminist options in order to create visions for the future from these interconnections. A feminist critical hermeneutics enables us to make choices between oppressive and liberating traditions of the Bible without having to accept or reject it as a whole. In this process of feminist critical evaluation and assessment, the Bible no longer functions as authoritative source but as a *resource* for women's struggle for liberation. Since the Bible is the model for Christian life and community, a feminist critical interpretation must explore *all* dimensions of the text and its traditions as well as its contemporary functions in order to assess their influence on women today, whether they are members of the church of women or not. A feminist paradigm of critical interpretation is not based on a faithful adherence to biblical texts or obedient submission to biblical

authority but on solidarity with women of the past and
present whose life and struggles are touched by the role of
the Bible in Western culture.

III. Toward a Feminist Model of Biblical Interpretation

To make the systematically articulated feminist experience
of the church of women central to biblical interpretation
and theological reflection requires a paradigm shift in
biblical interpretation, a shift from understanding the
Bible as archetypal myth to understanding it as historical
prototype. In the context of this paradigm shift a feminist
model of critical interpretation is emerging. This interpretive model of a critical feminist theology of liberation is in
the process of developing the following four structural elements which seem to emerge as constitutive for a feminist
biblical interpretation.

Since all biblical texts are formulated in androcentric
language and reflect patriarchal social structures, a feminist critical interpretation begins with a *hermeneutics of
suspicion* rather than with a hermeneutics of consent and
affirmation. It develops a *hermeneutics of proclamation*
rather than a hermeneutics of historical factualness, because the Bible still functions as Holy Scripture in Christian communities today. Rather than reducing the liberating impulse of the Bible to a feminist principle or one
feminist biblical tradition, it develops a *hermeneutics of
remembrance* that moves from biblical texts about women
to the reconstruction of women's history. Finally, this
model moves from a hermeneutics of disinterested distance
to a *hermeneutics of creative actualization* that involves
the church of women in the imaginative articulation of
women's biblical story and its ongoing history and community. Let us examine each of these four in detail.

A *hermeneutics of suspicion* does not presuppose the
feminist authority and truth of the Bible, but takes as its
starting point the assumption that biblical texts and their
interpretations are androcentric and serve patriarchal functions. Since most of the biblical writings are ascribed to
male authors and most of the biblical interpreters in

church and academy are men, such an assumption is justified. Just as the woman in the parable sweeps the whole house in search of her lost coin, so feminist critical interpretation searches for the lost traditions and visions of liberation among its inheritance of androcentric biblical texts and their interpretations. In order to unearth a "feminist coin" from the biblical tradition it critically analyzes contemporary scholarly and popular interpretations, the tendencies of the biblical writers and traditioning processes themselves, and the theoretical models underlying contemporary biblical-historical and theological interpretations.

In recent years feminist scholarship has cleared away many androcentric mistranslations, patriarchal interpretations, and one-sided reconstructions. The recovered material includes maternal God-language in Old Testament, the result of work by Phyllis Trible in particular, women's apostleship and leadership in the early Christian movement, which I have underlined, and the leadership of women in the ancient synagogue, which Bernadette Brooten has retrieved. Feminist critical scholarship has also pointed to the androcentric tendencies and patriarchal interest of biblical writers and of the canonization process in the so-called patristic period. Such tendencies can be traced, for example, in the different Old Testament references to the prophet Myriam, or in the way Luke plays down the apostleship of women and the writer of the Pastorals reintroduces a patriarchal model of biblical community, or in the canonical exclusion of traditions of so-called heretical movements.

A feminist hermeneutics of suspicion also questions the underlying presuppositions, androcentric models, and unarticulated interests of contemporary biblical interpretation. The very fact that we study only the statements of biblical writers about women but not about men reflects an androcentric theoretical-cultural paradigm that understands man as the paradigmatic human being and woman as the "other," the exception but not the rule. Biblical scholarship thus reproduces the effects of biblical language that generally subsumes woman under the generic *man* and *he*. Because scholars do not recognize the dynamics of this interpretive model of androcentrism, they do not understand that all androcentric language must be understood as generic language until proven otherwise. All androcentric biblical texts must therefore be assumed to speak about men and women unless women and female aspects are explicitly excluded.

The hermeneutics of suspicion thus has far-reaching consequences for the question of biblical translation, which has received much attention in recent years. The emotional reactions to the proposal of an inclusive translation indicate the political importance of this issue. If it is true that "the limits of our language are the limits of our world," then androcentric biblical language and its translation become a feminist issue of the utmost importance. Such language not only makes women marginal but also makes us invisible in the written classics of our culture, among which the Bible is preeminent.

An adequate biblical translation must render androcentric language differently at a time when androcentric language no longer is understood as generic language. Faithfulness to the biblical texts means translating those texts that are patriarchal with grammatically masculine language, and those texts that are not with grammatically feminine and masculine terms or with generic inclusive words. Therefore, a critical translation requires a feminist critical assessment and evaluation of the patriarchal oppressive or generic liberating dynamics of individual texts. A historically adequate translation must not present biblical generic texts as patriarchal on the one hand or veil their patriarchal character in generic language on the other hand. Feminist linguists have given us some guidelines for recognizing when language functions in a sexist way: Sexist language creates the linguistic invisibility or marginality of women; it describes women as dependent and as derived from men; it characterizes women in stereotypical roles and images; it ridicules women and trivializes their contributions; it mentions women only when they are the exceptions or present a problem; and it singles them out from other groups when it refers to "blacks, Jews, or Third World peoples, and women" as if women did not belong to each of these groups. A hermeneutics of suspicion must test not just the original biblical text but also contemporary translations for the presence of linguistic sexism.

While a historically adequate translation of the Bible brings to the fore the sexist-patriarchal as well as the feminist inclusive character of biblical texts, a hermeneutics of proclamation assesses the Bible's theological significance and power for the contemporary community of faith. Faithfulness to the struggle of women for liberation requires a theological judgment and an insistence that oppressive patriarchal texts and sexist traditions cannot claim the authority of divine revelation. Oppressive texts and traditions must be denounced as androcentric articulations of patriarchal interests and structures, and tested for their sexism, racism, and colonial militarism. This historical-critical assessment must be complemented by a political-critical feminist evaluation to assess the interaction of patriarchal biblical texts with contemporary culture. Rather than freeing women from cultural stereotypes and oppression, patriarchal texts reinforce cultural stereotypes and patriarchal submission. They do so not because they are misinterpreted but because they are formulated in order to legitimate patriarchal oppression.

Feminist-neutral or even feminist-positive texts of the Bible can also function to reinforce patriarchal sturctures if they are proclaimed or taught in order to assure patriarchal behavior and inculcate oppressive values. For example, if a battered woman is told to take up her cross and to suffer as Jesus did in order to save her marriage, then the feminist-neutral biblical motives are used to reinforce patriarchal values. Similarly, in a culture that socializes primarily women to altruism and selfless love, the biblical commandment of love and the call for service can be misused to sustain women's patriarchal exploitation. A feminist hermeneutics of proclamation must therefore analyze the role of biblical texts in contemporary patriarchal culture.

In conclusion, a feminist hermeneutics of proclamation must on the one hand insist that all texts identified as sexist or patriarchal should not be retained in the lectionary and be proclaimed in Christian worship or catechesis. On the other hand, those texts that are identified as transcending their patriarchal contexts and as articulating a liberating vision of human freedom and wholeness should receive their proper place in the liturgy and teaching of the churches. In short a feminist critical translation of the Bible must be complemented by a careful theological evaluation of biblical texts and their oppressive or liberating impact in specific cultural situations.

A feminist hermeneutics of proclamation must be balanced by a critical hermeneutics of remembrance that recovers *all* biblical traditions through a historical-critical reconstruction of biblical history from a feminist perspective. Rather than relinquishing androcentric biblical texts and patriarchal traditions, a hermeneutics of remembrance seeks to utilize historical-critical analysis to move beyond the androcentric text to the history of women in biblical religion.[7] If feminist identity is based not on the experience of biological sex or on essential gender differences but on the common historical experience of women as collaborating or struggling participants in patriarchal culture and biblical history, then the reconstruction of early Christian history in a feminist perspective is not just a historical-critical but also a feminist-theological task. Feminist meaning cannot be derived only from the egalitarian surplus of androcentric texts, but must also be found in and through androcentric texts and patriarchal history.

Rather than abandoning the memory of our foresisters' sufferings and hopes in our patriarchal Christian past, a hermeneutics of remembrance *reclaims* their sufferings and struggles through the subversive power of the "remembered past." If the enslavement of people becomes total when their history is destroyed and solidarity with the dead is made impossible, than a feminist biblical hermeneutics of remembrance has the task of becoming a "dangerous memory"[8] that reclaims the visions and sufferings of the dead. This "subversive memory" not only keeps alive the sufferings and hopes of women in the biblical past, but also allows for a universal solidarity among women of the past, present, and future. The continuing challenge of the victims of religious patriarchy is not met by a denial of their self-understanding and religious vision as mistaken or as ideological self-deception, but only through solidarity and committed remembrance of their hopes and despairs in the church of women.

A feminist hermeneutics of remembrance proposes theoretical models for historical reconstructions that place women in the center of biblical community and theology. Insofar as androcentric biblical texts not only reflect their patriarchal-cultural environment but also allow a glimpse of the early Christian movements as the discipleship of equals, the reality of women's commitment and leadership in these movements precedes the patriarchal injunctions of the New Testament. Although the canon only preserves remnants of a nonpatriarchal Christian ethos, these remnants indicate that such a "patriarchalization" process was not inherent in Christian community but progressed slowly and with difficulty. A feminist hermeneutics of remembrance can therefore reclaim early Christian theology and history as our own theology and history. Women as church have a continuous history and tradition that can claim the discipleship of equals as its biblical roots.

In short, a feminist hermeneutics of remembrance has as its primary task to keep alive the *memoria passionis* of biblical women as well as to reclaim our biblical heritage. This heritage is misrepresented when it is understood solely as a history of patriarchal oppression; it must also be reconstituted as a history of liberation and religious agency. The history and theology of women's oppression perpetuated by patriarchal biblical texts and clerical patriarchy must be understood for what they are. The history and theology must not be allowed to cancel out the memory of the struggle, life, and leadership of biblical women who spoke and acted in the power of the Spirit.

Historical reconstructions of women's biblical history need to be supplemented by a hermeneutics of creative actualization that expresses the active engagement of women in the ongoing biblical story of liberation. Whereas a feminist heremeneutics of remembrance is interested in historical-critical reconstruction, a feminist hermeneutics of creative actualization allows women to enter the biblical story with the help of historical imagination, artistic recreation, and liturgical ritualization. A feminist biblical interpretation therefore must be not only critical but also constructive, oriented not only toward the past but also toward the future of women-church.

A hermeneutics of creative actualization seeks to retell biblical stories from a feminist perspective, to reformulate biblical visions and injunctions in the perspective of the discipleship of equals, to create narrative amplifications of the feminist remnants that have survived in patriarchal texts. In this process of creative re-vision it utilizes all available means of artistic imagination—literary creativity, music, and dance. The Bible as formative prototype has inspired artistic creativity and legendary embellishments throughout the centuries. In midrash and apocryphal writings, in liturgy and sacred hymns, the patriarchal church has ritualized certain aspects of the biblical story and celebrated the "founding fathers" of biblical religion.

A feminist hermeneutics of creative actualization reclaims for the church of women the same imaginative freedom, popular creativity, and ritual powers. Women today not only rewrite biblical stories about women but also reformulate patriarchal prayers and create feminist rituals celebrating our ancestors. We rediscover in story and poetry, in drama and liturgy, in song and dance, our biblical foresisters' sufferings and victories. In feminist liturgy and celebrations women retell the story of the Passover or of the Last Supper; we re-vision the liturgy of advent or the baptismal ritual. In ever new images and symbols we seek to rename the God of the Bible and the significance of Jesus. We not only spin tales about the voyages of Prisca, the missionary, or about Junia, the apostle, but also dance Sarah's circle and experience prophetic enthusiasm. We sing litanies of praise to our foresisters and mourn the lost stories of our foremothers. Only by reclaiming our religious imagination and our sacred powers of naming can women-church "dream new dreams and see new visions."

We do so in the full awareness that creative participation in the biblical story must be won in and through a feminist critical process of interpretation that repents of the structural sin and internalized values of patriarchal sexism. The religious creativity and feminist power of ritualization actualized in the church of women seem to me the feminist "leaven" of the bakerwoman God that will transform patriarchal biblical religion, making the biblical story truly a resource for all who seek a sustaining vision in their struggle for liberation from patriarchal oppression.

2.

'For the Sake of Our Salvation . . .'
Biblical Interpretation and the
Community of Faith

THE RELATIONSHIP between the community of faith and biblical interpretation has become problematic and difficult. On the one hand, the Christian community claims the Bible to be canonical Holy Scripture for today; on the other hand, biblical scholarship has cast it more and more into the distant past and made it into a book fraught with complexities unintelligible to the ordinary believer.[1] The relationship between the Christian community and the Bible is thus characterized by the tension between the search for meaning in the contemporary situation and the historical particularity of the biblical texts.

The community of faith is generally concerned with contemporary questions of Christian faith and life style, and turns to the Bible in its search for answers and meaning. By contrast, the historical-critical approach of biblical scholarship underlines the specific historical character of biblical texts. Because it brings out the historically and culturally conditioned, and therefore limited, character of biblical statements, this approach emphasizes how remote and estranged the Scriptures are from the contemporary problems of the Christian community. This dilemma raises the fundamental theological question on how historically and culturally determined writings can have any theological significance and authority for contemporary persons and communities without losing their historical character and being transformed into ahistorical universal principles and timeless norms.

This deep cleft between the interests of the community of faith and those of historical biblical scholarship indicates a shift in theological paradigms. The category of paradigm used here evolved in the methodological debates of the natural sciences. According to Thomas S. Kuhn, a paradigm represents a coherent research tradition and creates a scientific community.[2] Since paradigms determine the ways in which scientists see the world, a shift in paradigm means a transformation of the scientific imagination and demands a basic "conversion" of the community of scientists. For instance, a shift from Aristotelian to Newtonian physics or from Newtonian physics to relativity means a scientific revolution in which old data are seen in a completely new perspective. For a period of time different paradigms may be competing for the allegiance of the scientific community, until one paradigm replaces the other or gives way to a third.

The usefulness of this theory for theology and the community of faith is obvious. The theory shows the historically conditioned nature of all scientific investigation. It also maintains that a language of neutral observation is not possible, that all scientific investigation demands commitment and a community of persons dedicated to a particular perspective. Moreover, it helps us understand that theological approaches, like all other scientific theories, are not falsified but are often replaced, not because we find new "data," but because we find a new way of looking at old data.

It is obvious that the tensions and problems in the relationship of the community of faith to the Bible are today occasioned by such a shift in theological paradigms. Whereas traditionally the Bible was perceived as divine revelation and held canonical authority for the church, since the Enlightenment it has been studied as a collection of historical writings.[3] Because this new historical and value-neutral paradigm was developed in contrast to a doctrinal-orthodox understanding of the Bible, it did not completely win the allegiance of the Christian community, which often continues to adhere to the doctrinal paradigm. Since ministers are trained to study the Bible in terms of the historical-factual paradigm but are committed to the service of the church, which understands the Bible not as a historical work but as proclamation of the Word of God for today, they are especially caught in this paradigm shift. The hermeneutical discussion and the sociology of knowledge school in turn have questioned the historical-factual paradigm, and this has led to a new theological paradigm. This new paradigm has not yet replaced the other two because its pastoral-theological implications are not yet sufficiently recognized by theologians and ministers alike. Since all three paradigms currently compete for the allegiance of the community of faith, we must analyze them further.

I. The Doctrinal Paradigm: The Bible as the Word of God

This paradigm is concerned with the authority and claims to truth of the biblical text for the Church and Christian faith. It conceives of the authority and truth claims of the Bible in ahistorical, dogmatic terms. In its most consistent form it insists on the verbal inspiration and literal accuracy of these biblical books.[4] All the words of the Bible are inspired—those that pertain to faith and Christian living as well as those that relate to matters of history or to issues of the natural and social sciences. In this understanding the Bible not only communicates the Word of God but *is* the Word of God. The theological presupposition of this paradigm is expressed in the liturgy when it is announced after reading a biblical text, not that "This is the Word of the Lord in the words of Paul" or "in the words of the Fourth Gospel," but "This is the Word of the Lord." The Bible is not simply a record of revelation but revelation itself. Therefore it is directly binding and has absolute authority: The Bible becomes a miraculous, divine book.

On a popular level the Bible may function as a divine oracle. We are all familiar with the spiritual gesture in which one opens the Bible after praying, points with closed eyes to a verse, and accepts it as God's directive for the particular situation for which guidance is sought. This literalist understanding of Scripture promotes a certain consumer mentality. Just as we have instant coffee without grinding the beans and filtering it, so we can have instant inspiration and guidance from the Bible without bothering with the obstacles of a historical understanding. The Bible becomes for many Christians a security blanket that provides ready-made answers to difficult existential and theological problems. In this popular approach to the Bible, the minister or preacher is the "mouthpiece" of God. In turn, he or she is in danger of preaching as the Word of God what is only his or her own word or prejudice.

In controversial theological questions, the Bible functions as proof text or first principle. The biblical books become a source of proof texts that are often taken out of context in order to legitimate predetermined dogmas, principles, or institutions of the Church. As such, reference to the Bible often takes the place of arguments for one's own position. The standing formula is "Scripture says, therefore . . . " Or "The Bible teaches, therefore we have to . . ." Such argument presupposes that the Bible reveals eternal truth and timeless principles, and thus biblical passages can justify the moral, doctrinal, or institutional interests of the church. This approach can include historical exegesis, in order to provide a more sophisticated argument.

A crass example of the misuse of exegetical argument is the Vatican statement against the ordination of women.[5] The document accepts the insight of New Testament scholarship that Jesus did not always follow the accepted norms of his culture; therefore, it argues, Jesus could have ordained women if he had wanted to. That he did not do so is a clear indication that Scripture is against the ordination of women. The argument appears completely logical. Yet it forgets to mention that New Testament scholarship seriously questions whether Jesus did ordain anyone to the priesthood as we understand ordination today.[6]

A variation of the proof text approach is the illustrative or theme approach, in which the biblical text is used to say something else. This allegorical mode of interpretation is one of the most traditional approaches to the Bible. Augustine's interpretation of the parable of the Good Samaritan illustrates this (*Quaest. Ev.* II. 19): A man (Adam) went from Jerusalem (state of original happiness) to Jericho (state of mortality). The robbers are the devil and his angels, the Samaritan is Christ, the inn is the Church, the innkeeper is not Peter but Paul; oil represents the comfort of hope, and wine the exhortation of faith. The allegorical approach, which uses the text to say something else, is often found today in modified form in systematic and practical theological reflection.[7]

The psychoanalytical approach understands the biblical text to symbolize or illustrate a psychological state. Although such an approach recognizes the validity of historical analysis, the analysis is not brought to bear on the third stage of reflection, where the distance between the subject and the object collapses into the fundamental question: How does the text resonate in us? The story of the healing of the paralytic (Mark 2:1-12) elicits questions like the following: Who is the "paralytic" in you? With what aspect of ourselves does this character resonate? Who is the "scribe" in you and what is the relationship of the "paralytic" and the "scribe" in you? "Now who are these four helpers? What resources are available to bring us to the healing value? What would it be like to marshal your paralytic and helpers to move to the healing source? That, after all, is what the story's about, isn't it?"[8] Here the historical text becomes a *chiffre* or illustration for an intrapsychological state and problem.

The illustrative approach is also found in the liturgical approach to Scripture. In the liturgy, the text stands as an illustration for a theological theme or statement. Insofar as the lectionary does not use only one reading but combines three quite disparate texts, it uses the Bible as a sourcebook for appropriate texts to reinforce a liturgical motif. The community of faith, whose only contacts with the Bible are often the sunday Scripture readings, thus never receives a comprehensive understanding of a biblical writing in its historical context or encounters a biblical book in its totality, but expreriences the Bible mainly as a proof or illustration for a theological theme or principle.

The preacher, on the other hand, is torn between the task of liturgical preaching and the approach of contemporary biblical scholarship, which insists that a text be understood in its wider context. The growing number of commentaries on the lectionary attempt to overcome this dilemma by providing scholarly and popular exegesis and pastoral suggestions, but fail to do so because the present structure of the liturgical readings does not allow the interpretation of a biblical text on its own grounds. This dilemma is aptly expressed in the following conversation between two preachers. "When I have found a text," says the first, "I always begin by studying the context in order to make sure of its original setting and meaning." "When I have found a text," replies his colleague, "I never look up the context for fear it will spoil the sermon."[9]

In short, this paradigm understands Scripture as verbally inspired, the direct revelation of God. As such Scripture reveals not only theological truth but also scientific truth. It provides us with infallible answers to our questions, with timeless principles for our actions, and with dogmatic guidelines for our theological reflection. But since church authority is aware that people have found and will continue to find different justifications for their own beliefs, it appropriates biblical interpretation for its own authority. The hierarchy and theologians as the representatives of the institutionalized church guard scriptural revelation and protect it from error. In this doctrinal paradigm Scripture is in danger of becoming an ideological justification for church doctrine and practice on the one hand, or personal edification and legitimization on the other. It is true that the Reformation attempted to recapture the critical potential of Scripture for the church and personal piety. Yet in Protestant orthodoxy biblical exegesis became again completely absorbed by dogmatics, providing proof texts for the doctrinal system.[10]

II. The Historical Paradigm:
The Bible as a Book of the Past

Historical criticism of the Bible evolved from confrontation with the dogmatic understanding of Scripture and the doctrinal authority of the church. Scholars with an objectivist, value-neutral, and rationalist understanding of history challenged the dogmatic interpretation of Scripture. Their understanding of exegesis was modeled after the natural sciences and attempted to create a purely objective reconstruction of the facts. As objectivist scientific historiography, this approach intended to unearth the historical data and therefore defined history as "what actually took place or happened." In this paradigm, theological meaning and truth thus become identified with historical factualness. If one is not able to establish a historical event as fact with objective accuracy, the event cannot be true. For example, if the Bible says that the world was created within a week, but natural science speaks of the evolution of the world and of humans in thousands of years, then the Bible is proven wrong and therefore not true.

In reaction to the historistic criticism of the Bible, Christian apologetics does not question the presuppositions of historistic criticism, but instead attempts to define the Bible on the same grounds. While radically rejecting historical criticism as dangerous for the faith, it nevertheless shares the historical contention that religious truth is identical with historical-factual truth.

Moreover, fundamentalist apologetics has linked the theological concept of inerrancy to the historistic understanding of truth.[11] Roman Catholicism shares in this fundamentalist Biblicism insofar as it is reluctant to accept biblical criticism and to free itself from precritical doctrinal positions.[12] This is probably one of the main reasons why serious historical-critical scholarship is not quite accepted in American Catholicism. Raymond Brown has pointed out that there is not one outstanding "first-class American Catholic graduate biblical school," and there is a general reluctance to investigate sensitive theological areas in the light of biblical criticism.[13]

Although the hermeneutical discussion has challenged the basic presuppositions of the historicist paradigm as inadequate for the interpretation of the Bible, ecclesiastical circles still operate with it. Moreover, although biblical historical scholarship is officially acknowledged by the Roman Catholic Church, religious educators and preachers are hesitant to disclose it to the community of faith, for fear that it would destroy the faith of the laity. When I asked my seminary students what they thought about the question we are discussing here, they confessed that they would be very hesitant to share exegetical insights and methods with the community of faith. Historical-critical insights can be digested by the clergy, but they do not belong in preaching and meditation. It is obvious that these students feel threatened by the scholarly interpretive approach to the Bible, because they were themselves reared under the historistic apologetic paradigm. Lay people, on the other hand, resent the fact that the clergy attempts to keep them uneducated in matters of biblical scholarship. For instance, when college students encounter the synoptic problem for the first time, their reaction is not so much to condemn the Bible as to condemn their parochial religious education for never mentioning this problem.

This reluctance to communicate historical-critical scholarship to the community of faith is not the result solely of fundamentalist clericalism, which considers the minister as the only "expert" on Scripture; it is also engendered by the self-understanding of exegetical scholarship. Although academic historical criticism has become suspicious of the objectivist-factual understanding of history, it still adheres to the dogma of a value-neutral, uninvolved historiography.[14] This approach studies the biblical texts, not as canonical texts of guiding importance for the community of faith, but as historical religious documents of Judaism and Christianity in antiquity or as Jewish and Christian literature of the Greco-Roman world. Since such a history of religions approach refuses to reconstruct the claims to faith of the biblical texts and to question their significance and authority today, it makes the canonical claims of Scripture obsolete. Historical-critical scholarship promoted in the academy reconstructs as objectively as possible the historical meaning of the text, but on methodological grounds refuses to discuss the significance of the biblical text for the community of faith today. The biblical interpreter becomes a historian of antiquity who is accountable to the academy but not to the community of faith. For fear of destroying the historical integrity of the Bible by making it relevant for today, scholars often make it so irrelevant that it loses all interest for anyone but the student of antiquity. Bible study is of the same order as the study of Homer or Virgil.

In this historical paradigm, exegetes understand themselves as historians of religion but not as theologians. The task of exegesis is to provide historical "data" for the theological reflections of systematic or moral theologians.[15] The task of biblical exegesis is to study the biblical text as a historical source that is part of ancient history, or to study it as literature and to discover the literary interest that shaped the text and what it meant to its original audience. The task of exegesis, is not to ask what the biblical text means for Christian and ecclesial self-understanding today; biblical interpretation is therefore limited to historical and literary inquiry, but, strictly speaking, is not a theological endeavor.

Since most American graduate departments that train future theologians and teachers operate under this paradigm, seminary teachers approach the Bible with the same perspective. They usually leave it to their ministerial students to bridge the gap between the exegetical-historical and the ministerial task. The minister is expected to become the mediator between value-neutral, historical exegesis and the church's commitment to the Bible as Scripture, between what the Bible meant and what it means today. Future ministers of the Word sense this disparity between their ministerial task and their exegetical training, but are often unable to pinpoint the problem accurately. Either they attempt to extend the university model of historical criticism into their pastoral work, or they forget what they have studied in seminary and graduate school and fall back into the doctrinal paradigm. Since they were taught a methodological procedure that consisted of a value-neutral historical exegesis as a first step, and theological or pastoral application as the second, not integrally related step, the temptation is great to relinquish laborious historical inquiry for the sake of ready-made piety or dogmatic interests.

This failure of biblical scholarship not only to seek the meaning of the text in its historical context but also to search for the significance of the text for us today is, in my opinion, one of the main reasons why historical-critical scholarship has such slight impact on the church community today. I recently attended a biblical conference where scholars bemoaned how little influence biblical scholarship has today on church policies and teachings. The next day, when a paper on women in early Christianity was read, the same scholars insisted that it does not make any difference whether or not Jesus preached a sexist gospel. As soon as historical-critical questions were raised in the context of a contemporary debate, the questions lost their scholarly interest because they were closely linked to a contemporary discussion within the church.

III. The Pastoral-Theological Paradigm[16]

If the Bible as a historical and canonical book is to gain more influence in the life of the contemporary church, then it is necessary to chart a new paradigm of biblical interpretation that would integrate the two competing paradigms that determine biblical interpretation today. This new paradigm must take seriously the methodological insights of historical-critical scholarship, but must also radically question whether neutral and uncommitted exegetical research is possible. Biblical interpretation cannot limit itself to working out what the author and the text *meant;* it must also critically elaborate what the theological significance of the text is for today. This new paradigm could be called pastoral-theological, for it holds the pastoral situation and the theological response to it, the historical and theological aspects, the past and the present, in creative tension. It understands the Bible, not as a conglomeration of doctrinal propositions or proofs, not as historical-factual transcripts, but as the model of Christian faith and life.

This new paradigm was prepared by two developments in biblical scholarship. The methods of form and redaction criticism have demonstrated how much the biblical writings are theological responses to pastoral, practical situations.[17] And the hermeneutical discussion has made obsolete a value-free, objectivist study of historical texts.[18] At the same time, critical theology has maintained that it is not sufficient to understand the historical meaning of biblical texts. What is also necessary is a critical evaluation of their ideological function within an ecclesial or social context.[19] Both perceptive understanding and critical judgment are necessary in order to set free the liberating traditions of the Bible and their significance for the community of faith today.

Content and Context

Form and redaction criticism have demonstrated that the biblical tradition is not a doctrinal or exegetical tradition, but a living tradition of the community of faith. In order to understand biblical texts, we must do more than analyze and understand the context of a given text; we must determine the situation and community to which this text is addressed. This is obvious when we study the Pauline letters. Whereas the Pauline literature was long seen as a compendium of the theological teaching and principles of Paul, scholars today understand them as letters and not as doctrinal handbooks. The letter of Paul to the Galatians could not have been written to the Corinthians and vice versa. Similarly, the Gospels were written for certain communities with specific problems and theological understandings. We must study both content and context.[20]

Form and source criticism have shown that the material of the biblical writers was collected, selected and formulated so that it could speak to the needs and situations of the community of faith. The materials and traditions about Jesus, for instance, were selected and reformulated so that they would have meaning for the Christian community that transmitted them. The early Christians were free in their use of the Jesus traditions; they changed or reformulated them and reinterpreted them by bringing them into a different context and framework. Matthew not only changes the form of Mark's text on the great commandment from a scholarly dialogue to a controversy dialogue but also reformulates the question.[21] In Mark the lawyer asks which commandment is the chief or first commandment; Matthew changes the question into one for the "key" to the law, in order to adapt the question to the Jewish discussion, where it was most important to know how one could do justice to the 613 commandments. Luke, on the other hand, connects the controversy dialogue of Mark with the story of the Good Samaritan and shifts the emphasis from knowing the commandments to doing them. Thus the Gospel writers were not content to repeat formulas and stories just because they belonged to the tradition; instead they reformulated them in order to respond to the needs of the Christians of their own day.

Despite the insights to be gained from this approach, form and redaction critical studies can be criticized for focusing too narrowly on the community and for conceptualizing the situation of the early Christian communities too strictly in terms of a confessional struggle between different theologies and church groups. Such a reconstruction often reads like the history of the European Reformation in the sixteenth century or a description of a small town in America where five or six churches of different denominations are built within walking distance of one another. We must recognize, therefore, not only that the early Christian writers responded to inner theological or inner church problems, but also that the early Christian communities were missionary communities deeply embedded in their own culture or critically distancing themselves from it.[22] The biblical writers transmit their faith response to the cultural and religious problems of their own time. They indicate that Christian faith can either adapt to or confront the given culture.

The studies of the social world of early Christianity underline that Christian faith and revelation are always intertwined with the cultural, political, and social contexts, and we can no longer neatly separate biblical revelation from its cultural expression.[23] It does not suffice to understand texts in religious-theological terms; it is also necessary to analyze their sociopolitical contexts and expression. For instance, while the historistic approach to the miracles of the New Testament discusses whether or not they actually could have happened or whether they happened as they are told, the historical-theological approach debates whether belief in miracles is a genuine Christian expression of faith or whether it shares too much in the magical beliefs of the times by presenting Jesus in analogy to the miracle workers of antiquity.

While the historical-theological understanding emphasizes a "heretical" Christian group as the proponent of
such crude miracle-faith, the societal interpretation of
miracles points out that miracle faith was widespread
among the lower classes, who were uneducated and did not
have money for medical treatment. The miracle stories,
therefore, strengthen the hope of those who were exploited and oppressed. For instance, the demon in Mark 5:1–13
is called Legion, the same name given the Roman soldiers
who occupied Palestine. The story presents an irony of the
Roman exploitation when it has the demon expelled into a
herd of pigs, animals that were, for Jewish sensitivities, the
essence of ritual impurity. Here miracle-faith is a protest
against physical political suffering. It gives courage to resist
all life-destroying power of one's society.

In sum, in reinterpreting their traditions, the biblical
writers do not follow the doctrinal or historistic paradigm
but rather the paradigm of pastoral or practical theology,
insofar as the concrete pastoral situation of the community determines selection, transmission, and creation of the
biblical traditions. The New Testament authors rewrote
their traditions in the form of letters, gospels, or apocalyp-
ses, because they felt theologically compelled to illuminate
or censure the beliefs and praxis of their communities. The
biblical books are thus written with the intention of serv-
ing the needs of the community of faith and not of revealing timeless principles or transmitting historically accurate
records. They therefore do not locate revelation only in
the past but also in their own present, thereby revealing a
dialectical understanding between present and past. The
past, on the one hand, is significant because revelation happened decisively in Jesus of Nazareth. On the other hand,
the writers of the New Testament can freely use the Jesus
traditions because they believe that the Jesus who spoke
then speaks now to his followers through the Holy Spirit.[24]

The relevance of this understanding of tradition for the
Scriptures is obvious. We have to learn that not all texts
speak to all situations and to everyone. It is therefore
necessary for the minister to learn how to determine the
situation and needs of his or her congregation with the

same sophistication he or she applies to the study of biblical texts. Moreover he or she must be aware of the sociological, psychological, cultural, and political influences that shape the world and self-understanding of the community of faith. A repetition of biblical texts does not suffice. For example, if a minister preached about the theology of grace expressed in Romans 9–11 during the time of the Nazis but did not speak about the gas chambers of Auschwitz and the annihilation of the Jewish people, that minister did not preach the gospel but perverted the biblical message. The pastoral-theological paradigm does not permit a mere repetition or application of biblical texts, but demands a translation of their meaning and context into our own situation.[25]

The Bible as Root-Model of the Christian Church

Historical-critical studies teach us that there is not one way of formulating Christian proclamation and theology or of building Christian communities and living as a Christian. The pastoral-theological paradigm therefore demands a redefinition of what the canon means.[26] The canon should not be viewed, as it is in the doctrinal paradigm, in an exclusive fashion as a negative judgment on all other early Christian writings that were not included by the church among the books of the New or Old Testament. Instead, the canon should be understood in an inclusive fashion as creating a multiform model of Christian church and Christian life. The canon includes not only the New Testament but also the Jewish Scriptures, not one Gospel but four, not only the Pauline letters but also James or Hebrews, not only Acts but also the Apocalypse, writings from Palestine and Asia Minor or Greece, addressed both to Jews and to Gentiles. It encompasses not only Matthean but also Johannine theology, not only apocalyptic but also realized eschatology.

This concept of the canon also has implications for our pastoral-theological practice today, for it demands that we distinguish more carefully between preaching or proclamation and teaching or catechesis. If the canon presents the root-model of Christian community and faith, then we are bound to explore all dimensions of this model. Whereas the task of preaching is to select those biblical texts that address the questions of the contemporary community, the task of teaching is to preserve the multiplicity of the early Christian traditions and communities. The task of teaching is to transmit all the biblical traditions, whether they are meaningful and relevant to a specific situation of a Christian community or not. In some situations it would be wrong to proclaim certain biblical traditions, and at some time one is not able to do more than keep the traditions of biblical faith. We cannot preach all traditions because we do not really understand them or they do not come alive for us. Yet we have to keep and preserve them because we are aware of the danger of destroying the multiform root model of the biblical canon.

The interrelation between teaching and preaching should not be understood to mean that the teacher has to preserve objective biblical historical data and the preacher or theologian has to apply these data to a contemporary situation or problem. Nor does it mean that the teacher approaches the Bible in a value-neutral, scientific attitude, whereas the preacher must be committed to the Christian community and its interests. Such an objectivist and value-neutral stance of the teacher would conflict with the very intention of the New Testament books themselves.

Moreover, the hermeneutical discussion has pointed out that an objectivist, value-free historiography and exegesis are not possible, since the interpreter always approaches the text with specific questions or with a specific way of raising questions, and thus with a certain understanding of the issues with which the text is concerned.[27] The interpreter's mind is not a *tabula rasa*, but before we attempt to understand how an author deals with a given subject and before we can get interested in a text, we must have a certain common interest, understanding, or life-relation, to the issues of which the text speaks. Just as we need an appreciation of music in order to understand a textbook on musicology, so must the biblical interpreter have a certain relationship to the community of faith and to the religious questions raised by it if he or she wants to grasp the intention and subject matter of these texts.

In other words, understanding takes place in a circular movement: Interpretation and answer are to some extent determined by the question, which in turn is confirmed, extended, or corrected by the text. A new question then grows out of this understanding, so that the hermeneutical circle continues to develop in a never-ending spiral.[28] Therefore, understanding a text depends as much on the questions and presuppositions of the interpreter as on material explanation.[29] The interpreter committed to understanding the text is prepared to have his or her presuppositions corrected if necessary. By contrast, illegitimate prejudice refuses to alter its preconceived judgment when new insights are derived from the text and thus reduces the hermeneutical spiral to a vicious circle. Such presuppositions and prejudices of the interpreter or of a theological school are psychologically, socially, and culturally determined.

These insights of the hermeneutical discussion have far-reaching consequences for the study and interpretation of the Bible within the community of faith. Students of the Bible should be trained not only to correctly analyze historical texts and literary forms but also to reflect methodologically on their own presuppositions or prejudices as well as on those of scholarly interpretations. It is obvious in this context how damaging it is that almost all biblical scholars are middle-class, white males who are highly educated and belong to the clergy. It is essential to break the monopoly of this class if the Bible is to truly become again Scripture for the community of faith. It is absolutely mandatory that people of different life styles, social backgrounds, and personal experience become involved in the interpretation of Scripture.[30] An involvement of people with different experiences and perceptions will generate new questions in biblical interpretation.

Biblical scholars must not only discuss the questions raised by the historical scholarship of their colleagues but also pay attention to the questions and discoveries of the community of faith.[31] The task of biblical scholarship is therefore not only historical scientific research but also scholarly validation or rejection of the questions raised by the communities of faith that respond to the historical biblical text always on the basis of their own Christian experience. Biblical interpretation and preaching are not possible without listening to the experiences of very different people. Just as preachers can no longer afford to prepare a sermon on a biblical text in the seclusion of the study without having discussed it with a group of people beforehand,[32] so biblical scholars must address the questions of the community of faith if they are to be of service to the Christian community.

Revelation 'For the Sake of Our Salvation'

If we take seriously the position that the biblical writings are pastoral-theological responses to the situations and problems of their own times and communities, then we have to expect that not all writings are of theological significance for us today. A hermeneutics of consent to the historical-theological meaning of the biblical texts does not suffice.[33] We must both understand these texts and evaluate them theologically. For instance, in the face of the all-destructive powers of modern warfare, we must ask whether we still can pray the curses of the Old Testament psalms against the enemies of Israel. Feminist theology questions whether we can repeat the patriarchal biblical language for God today, and political theology doubts that biblical texts that speak of God as an absolute monarch are still adequate. What is necessary for theological interpretation today, therefore, is not only an understanding of their historical-theological meaning but also a critical-theological evaluation of their functions in the history of the church and in the contemporary church.

The need for a critical evaluation of various biblical texts and traditions was always recognized within the Christian church. While the doctrinal paradigm selected those passages of Scripture that supported ecclesiastical doctrine, the historical paradigm evaluated the theological truth of biblical texts according to their historicity. The pastoral-theological paradigm has to define the canon as the inclusive root-model of Christian church, stressing the canon includes various, often contradictory theological responses to historical situations of the early Christian communities.[34] Since not all New Testament responses are of equal theological quality, and not all can equally express Christian revelation, New Testament scholarship attempts to find theological criteria or a "canon within the canon" in order to evaluate the various early Christian traditions.[35] The doctrinal paradigm formulated this sort of canon after the model of revelatory essence and historical expression, timeless truth and culturally conditioned language, or constant tradition and changing traditions. When the "canon within the canon" is formulated along the lines of the historical paradigm, scholars juxtapose Jesus and Paul, Pauline theology and early Catholicism, the historical Jesus and the early church. Divine revelation and truth are, in this perspective, identified with the earliest historically verifiable traditions.[36]

The pastoral-theological paradigm has to formulate its own criterion, which cannot be derived from biblical texts but must be drawn from Christian communities, to which these texts speak today. The criterion does not measure the theological validity of biblical texts, for their own communities, but evaluates them according to the theological insights and questions of the Christian community today. For example, the Constitution on Divine Revelation of Vatican II acknowledges that Scripture "*contains* revelation, namely, in the form of a written record; but that not all of Scripture *is* revelation."[37] It follows Augustine and Thomas in formulating a criterion that limits revealed truth and inerrancy to matters pertaining to the salvation of the Christian and human community. "Therefore, since everything asserted by the inspired authors or sacred writers must be held to be asserted by the Holy Spirit, it follows that the books of Scripture must be acknowledged as teaching firmly, faithfully, and without error that truth which God wanted put into the sacred writings *for the sake of our salvation*" [emphasis added].[38]

Salvation here should not be understood just as salvation of the soul, but in the biblical sense of total human salvation and wholeness. It cannot be limited to the liberation from sin, but must be understood to mean also liberation from social and political oppression. Conversely, oppressive and destructible biblical traditions cannot be acknowledged as divine revelation. For example, feminist theology has pointed out that women are oppressed and exploited by patriarchal and sexist structures and institutions. Therefore, according to this criterion, biblical revelation and truth can today be found only in those texts and traditions that transcend and criticize the patriarchal culture and religion of their times. A pastoral-theological interpretation of the Bible concerned with the truth and meaning of Scripture in a postpatriarchal culture and society must maintain that only the nonsexist traditions of the Bible present divine revelation if the Bible is not to become a tool for the further oppression of women.

A critical scrutiny and evaluation of biblical texts according to whether or not they contribute to the salvation, well-being, and freedom of women should not be understood in terms of the doctrinal essence and historical relativity model, as though we were able to separate culturally conditioned, patriarchal expression from a timeless nonsexist essence of revelation. It should also not be understood in terms of the pristine beginnings-deterioration model, as though nonpatriarchal traditions are limited to the earliest traditions of the New Testament. Such a critical criterion of evaluation must be applied to *all* biblical texts in order to determine how much they contribute to the "salvation" or oppression of women.[39]

I have proposed here that the difficulties of the community of faith with the Bible are engendered by the rivalry of three different paradigms of interpretation. Ecclesial pronouncements and popular fundamentalism often follow the doctrinal paradigm, and the study of the Bible in the academy is determined by the historical paradigm. A third paradigm has emerged, that I have here characterized as pastoral-theological. Thomas S. Kuhn has pointed out that a new scientific paradigm must create a new scientific community with common interests, journals, and channels of communication if it is to replace the preceding one. The doctrinal paradigm is represented by the teaching authority of the church, and the historical paradigm is situated in the academy; the emerging pastoral-theological paradigm has not yet engendered its own communal structurers. At present the institutional basis of this paradigm is the seminary or academic departments of religion, whereby the seminary educates future ministers of the faith and the academy educates future scholars and teachers of religion in antiquity.

As long as the pastoral-theological paradigm of biblical interpretation does not lead to its own American institutional basis, we will not be able to escape the present dilemma of biblical interpretation. Centers of pastoral-theological interpretation could gather together a scientific community and facilitate the cooperation of biblical scholars, of priests and ministers, and of the active members of the community of faith in studying the Bible. Such centers would have to explore scientifically not only the historical meaning of biblical texts but also the doctrinal interests of the institutionalized churches, the presuppositions of academic historiography, and the needs and situations of the contemporary community of faith in its sociopolitical context. Involved in such pastoral-theological biblical centers could be persons from different churches and communities, from different races, classes, sexes, ages, and cultures, from different professions and educational backgrounds.

These centers would have to integrate historical-theological scholarship and the contemporary theological needs and insights of the community of faith in order to say God's word in a new language, so that the Bible will contribute to the "salvation" of contemporary people. Their task would not be inspirational popularization and pious application of the biblical text to our own situation but rigorous intellectual theological scholarship committed to the needs of the community of faith. The beginnings of a new scientific community of the pastoral-theological paradigm already exist all over the country in task forces and study groups dedicated to the pastoral-theological interpretation of the Bible.

3.

The Function of Scripture in the Liberation Struggle
A Critical Feminist Hermeneutics and Liberation Theology

TO DISCUSS the relationship between liberation theology and biblical interpretation in general, and to consider the function of the Bible in the struggle of women for liberation in particular, is to enter an intellectual and emotional mine field. One must detect and uncover the contradictions between historical exegesis and systematic theology, between value-free scientific inquiry and "advocacy" scholarship, between universal-objectivist preconceptions of academic theology and the critical partiality of liberation theologies. To attempt this in a short chapter entails, by necessity, a simplification and classification of a complex set of theological problems.

To raise the issue of the contemporary meaning and authority of the Bible from a feminist theological perspective, and to do this from the marginal position of a woman in the academy, is to expose oneself to triple jeopardy.[1] Establishment academic theologians and exegetes will reject such an endeavor as unscientific, biased, and overly conditioned by contemporary questions and therefore unhistorical, or they will refuse to accept it as a serious exegetical or theological question because the issue is raised by a woman. Liberation and political theologians will, at best, consider such a feminist theological endeavor as one problem among others, or at worst label it middle class and peripheral to the struggle of oppressed people. After all, how can middle-class white women worry about the Equal Rights Amendment (ERA) or the sex of God when people are dying of starvation, being tortured in prisons, or barely subsisting in the black and Hispanic ghettos of American cities? This kind of objection against feminist theology and the women's movement overlooks the fact that more than half of the poor and hungry in the world are women and children dependent on women.[2] Women and children represent the majority of the "oppressed," and poor and Third World women must bear the triple burden of sexism, racism, and classism. If liberation theologians make the "option for the oppressed" the key to their theological endeavors, then they must articulate that "the oppressed" are women.

Feminist theology challenges academic theology to take its own intellectual presuppositions seriously, and asks other liberation theologies to specify their option for the oppressed. The feminist theologian challenges the supposedly neutral and objective stance of academic theologians, but also qualifies the definition of the advocacy stance of liberation theology as "option for the oppressed." Her involvement in liberation theology is not "altruistic," but based on the acknowledgment and analysis of her own oppression as a woman in sexist, cultural, and theological institutions. Having recognized the dimensions of her own oppression, she can no longer advocate the value-neutral, detached stance of the academician. In other words, feminist theologians' experience of oppression is different from that of Latin American theologians, for instance, who often do not belong to the poor, but have made the cause of the oppressed their own.[3] This emphasis on the differences in the approaches of different liberation theologies is important. As Robert McAfee Brown has pointed out, "What we see depends on where we are standing."[4]

The Native American theologian Vine Deloria has cautioned that one way of co-opting liberation theology is to classify all minorities as oppressed and in need of liberation.[5] Christian theologians often add to this that we are all under sin and therefore all equally oppressed: male and female, black, white, and red. In co-opting the term *oppression* and generalizing it so that it becomes meaningless, the liberal establishment successfully neutralizes specific analyses of oppression and prohibits oppressed groups from formulating their own goals and strategies for liberation. Therefore, we cannot speak about oppression in generalized terms or about liberation theology in the singular.

I. The Advocacy Stance of Liberation Theologies

This insight has far-reaching consequences for the methodological approach of this chapter. Instead of seeking the scriptural *loci* of liberation theology in general, or critically evaluating their approach from a "superior" methodological historical-critical point of view, I shall concentrate on one issue of concern to both academic theology and all forms of liberation theology. The basic insight of liberation theologies and their methodological starting point is that all theology knowingly or not is by definition always engaged for or against the oppressed. Intellectual neutrality is not possible in a historical world of exploitation and oppression. If this is the case, then theology cannot talk about human existence in general, or about biblical theology in particular, without identifying whose human existence is meant and whose God is found in biblical symbols and texts.

This avowed advocacy stance of all liberation theologies seems to be the major point of contention between academic historical-critical or liberal-systematic theology on the one side and liberation theology on the other side. For instance, in many exegetical and theological circles a feminist interpretation of the Bible or the reconstruction of early Christianity is not the proper substantive historical and theological subject matter for serious academic theology. Since such a feminist interpretation is sparked by the women's movement and openly confesses its allegiance to it, academic theologians consider it be a fad, and not a serious historical-theological problem for historical-critical scholarship.[6] Since this interpretive approach is already prejudiced by the explicit advocacy position of the inquiring scholar, no value-free scientific inquiry is possible. Therefore, no one publicly identified with the "feminist cause" in theology and society can be considered a "serious" scholar. Or as one of my colleagues remarked about a professor who wrote a rather moderate article on women in the Old Testament, "It's a shame! In writing this article she may have ruined her whole scholarly career." The ideal of historical-critical studies, that all exegetical inquiry should be a value-neutral and objective historical description of the past, overlooks the fact that biblical studies as *canonical* studies are already "engaged," for the Bible is not just a document of past history, but functions as Holy Scripture in Christian communities today.[7] The *biblical* exegete and theologian, in contrast to the historian of antiquity, never searches solely for the historical meaning of a passage, but also raises the question of the Bible's meaning and authority for today. The contention that "hermeneutical privilege of the oppressed" or the feminist interest in the role of women in the New Testament is too engaged or biased pertains, therefore, to all biblical inquiry *qua* biblical inquiry, and not only to the study and use of the Bible by liberation theologians.[8] Insofar as biblical studies are "canonical" studies, they are related to and inspired by their *Sitz im Leben* in the Christian church past and present. The feminist analysis of the Bible is just one example of an ecclesial context and of the theological commitment of biblical studies in general.

This fact is recognized by Schubert Ogden, who nevertheless objects to the advocacy stance of liberation theology. He argues that all existing liberation theologies are in danger of becoming ideologies in the Marxist sense insofar as, like other traditional theological enterprises, they are "the rationalization of positions already taken."[9] Rather than engaging in a critical reflection on their own positions, liberation theologies rationalize, with the help of the Bible, the positions of the oppressed instead of those of the oppressors. Insofar as they attempt to rationalize the prior claims of Christian faith and their own option for the oppressed, they are not theologizing but witnessing. Theology as a "second act" exists according to Latin American liberation theologians, not "for its own sake," but for the sake of the church's witness, its liberating praxis.

One must question whether this statement adequately characterizes the advocacy stance of liberation theologians. Ogden suggests that the only way theology—be it academic or liberation theology—can become emancipated is by conceiving its task as that of a critical reflection on its own position. He then proceeds to work out a "still more adequate theology of liberation than any of them has as yet achieved."[10] But he fails to reflect critically on the political standpoint and implications of his own process theology, and he goes on to talk about "women's theology" and to explore the "being of God in himself" as if he had never studied feminist theology.

Whereas Ogden accuses liberation theologians of too "provincial an understanding of bondage," James Cone insists to the contrary that the option for the oppressed should become the starting point of all theology: "If Christian theology is an explication of the meaning of the gospel for our time, must not theology itself have liberation as its starting point or run the risk of being, at best, idle talk, and at worst blasphemy?"[11] Such a provocative formulation should not be classified as mere "rhetoric."[12] Instead it must be seen as an indicator of serious theological differences in the understanding of the task and function of theology.

The disagreement over the function and goal of theology has serious implications for the way theologians understand the task of biblical interpretation. As a feminist theologian I have taken the advocacy position, but I do not think that this option excludes "critical reflection" on my own feminist position. Critical reflection must be applied both to the advocacy position of liberation theologies and to the ways exegetes and theologians have construed the relationship between the biblical past and its meanings, and explicated the claim of Christian theology that the Bible has authority and significance for Christians today.

In order to reflect critically on the function of liberation theologians' explicit advocacy position in the process of biblical theological interpretation, I will discuss here two concrete examples of liberation theological hermeneutics. This is necessary because it is methodologically incorrect to reduce every advocacy stance and every analysis of concrete structures of oppression by liberation theologies to one common level. I will argue that liberation theologies, because of their option for a specific group of oppressed people, such as women or Native Americans, must develop within the overall interpretive approach of a critical theology of liberation more adequate heuristic interpretive models appropriate to specific forms of oppression. In short, the biblical interpretation of liberation theologians must become more concrete, or more "provincial," before an "interstructuring" of different interpretive models and a more universal formulation of the task of a critical theology of liberation can be attemped.

Thomas S. Kuhn's categories of scientific paradigms and heuristic models, which evolved in the methodological discussion of the natural sciences, provide a conceptual theoretical framework that allows for the advocacy stance of liberation theologies, as well as for their distinctive interpretive approaches.[13] Kuhn's theory of paradigms shows the conditioned nature of all scientific investigation, and demonstrates that no neutral observation language or value-free standpoint is possible, since all scientific investigations demand commitment to a particular research approach and are carried out by a community of scholars dedicated to such a theoretical perspective. Moreover, this theory helps us to understand that theological approaches, like all other scientific theories, are not falsified but replaced not because we find new "data," but because we find new ways of looking at old data and problems. Research paradigms are therefore not necessarily exclusive of each other. They can exist alongside each other until they are finally replaced by a new paradigm.

The debate surrounding the advocacy stance of liberation theology and the value-neutral stance of academic theology appears to reflect a shift in theological paradigms. Since the Bible as Holy Scripture is a historical book, but at the same time claims to have significance and authority for Christians today, theological scholarship has developed different paradigms to resolve the tension between the historical and theological claims of the Bible.[14]

Chapter 2 elaborated that all three paradigms of biblical interpretation espouse a definite stance and allegiance to a research perspective and community. The doctrinal paradigm clearly has its allegiance to the church and its teachings. The norm by which it evaluates different texts and their truth claims is the *regula fidei*. The scientific paradigm of historical-critical exegesis shares in the objectivist-scientific worldview and espouses the critical rationality and value-free inquiry of academic scholarship. The hermeneutic-contextual paradigm is interested in the "continuation" of the tradition and therefore advocates a position in line with neo-orthodox theology, a "hermeneutics of consent."[15] It would be interesting to explore which political interests each of these paradigms serves, but this would go far beyond the task and aim of this chapter. The explicit advocacy position, however, of liberation theologies threatens to uncover these hidden political interests of existing biblical interpretive paradigms. This may be one of the main reasons established theology refuses to reflect critically on its own social-ecclesial interests and political functions.

II. Liberation Theology and Biblical Interpretation

The main part of this chapter will explore critically the position of a theology of liberation within the existing paradigms of biblical interpretation. It will do this by discussing two different hermeneutical approaches of liberation theologies. As case studies, I have chosen the hermeneutical model of Juan Luis Segundo, and have placed this in contrast to Elizabeth Cady Stanton's approach in proposing *The Woman's Bible*. Both examples indicate that liberation theologies have worked out a distinctive approach to biblical interpretation that leads to a redefinition of the criteria for public theological discourse. Instead of asking whether an approach is appropriate to the Scriptures and adequate to the human condition,[16] one needs to test whether a theological model of biblical interpretation is *adequate* to the historical-literary methods of contemporary interpretation and *appropriate* to the struggle of the oppressed for liberation.

The Interpretative Model of Juan Luis Segundo

While the hermeneutic-contextual approach advocates the elimination of all presuppositions and preunderstandings for the sake of objective-descriptive exegesis, existential hermeneutics defines preunderstanding as the common

existential ground between the interpreter and the author
of the text. Political theologians have challenged this
choice of existential philosophy, while liberation theologians maintain a hermeneutics of engagement instead of a
hermeneutics of detachment. Since no complete detachment or value-neutrality is possible, the interpreter must
make her or his stance explicit and take an advocacy position in favor of the oppressed. To truly understand the
Bible is to read it through the eyes of the oppressed, since
the God who speaks in the Bible is the God of the oppressed. For a correct interpretation of the Bible, it is
necessary to acknowledge the "hermeneutical privilege
of the oppressed" and to develop a hermeneutics "from
below."

Since theology is explicitly or implicitly intertwined
with the existing social situation, according to Segundo[17]
the hermeneutic circle must begin with an experience or
analysis of the social reality that leads to suspicion about
our real situation. At the second level we apply our ideological suspicion to theology and to all other ideological
superstructures. At a third level we experience theological
reality in a different way, which in turn leads us to the suspicion that "the prevailing interpretation of the Bible has
not taken important pieces of data into account."[18] At the
last level we bring these insights to bear upon the interpretation of Scripture. Only active commitment to the
oppressed and active involvement in their struggle for
liberation enable us to see our society and our world differently, and give us a new perspective for looking at the
world. This perspective is also taught in the New Testament if the latter is interpreted correctly.

Segundo notes that James Cone has elaborated such a
liberation theological interpretation for the black community, and acknowledges his indebtedness to Bultmann,
but he reformulates the hermeneutic circle to include
action.

And the circular nature of this interpretation stems
from the fact that each new reality obliges us to interpret the Word of God afresh, to *change* reality accordingly, and then go back and reinterpret the Word of
God again and so on [emphasis added].[19]

It is apparent that Segundo cannot be accused of rationalizing a previously taken position. He does not operate within the interpretive traditions of the doctrinal paradigm. He also clearly distinguishes his own theological interpretation from that of academic historical-critical scholarship by rejecting the biblical revelation-contemporary application model. According to him biblical interpretation must reconstruct the second-level learning process of biblical faith. Faith is identical with the total process of learning through ideologies, whereas the responses of faith to certain historical situations are ideologies. Therefore, faith should not be defined as content or *depositum fidei*, but as an educational process throughout biblical and Christian history. Faith expresses the continuity and permanence of divine revelation, whereas ideologies document the historical character of faith and revelation. "Faith then is a liberative process. It is converted into freedom *for ideologies*."[20] It is obvious that Segundo does not understand ideology as "false" consciousness, but as historical-societal expression.

According to him, Christian faith is also not to be defined as content, doctrine, or principle, but as an educational process to which we willingly entrust ourselves. "In the case of . . . the Bible we learn by entrusting our life and its meaning to the historical process that is reflected in the expressions embodied in that particular tradition."[21] It is clear that Segundo does not work within the overall approach of either the doctrinal or historical value-free paradigms, but proposes an interpretive model within the hermeneutic-contextual paradigm. He shares with neo-orthodoxy the hermeneutical presupposition that scriptural traditions are meaningful, and that they can therefore claim our obedience and demand a "hermeneutics of consent." In contrast to neo-orthodox theology, Segundo does not claim that meaning and liberation are found in the *content* of Scripture but rather in the process of learning how to learn.

This proposal does not consider that both the content of Scripture and the second-level learning process can be distorted. Segundo must, therefore, either demonstrate that this is not the case, or formalize this learning process so that the advocacy stance becomes an abstract principle not applicable to the contents of the Bible. In other words, Segundo's model does not allow for a critical theological evaluation of biblical ideologies as "false consciousness." One must question whether historical content and hermeneutic learning can be separated. Such a proposal also does not allow us to judge whether a text or interpretation is appropriate and helpful to the struggle of the oppressed for liberation. The failure to bring a critical evaluation to bear upon the biblical texts *and* upon the process of interpretation within Scripture and tradition is one reason liberation thelogians' use of the Bible often approximates that of scholars who seek texts as proof of their position. To avoid this, liberation hermeneutics must reflect on the fact that the process of interpretation of Scripture is not necessarily liberative.

The Interpretive Model of
Elizabeth Cady Stanton

While liberation theologians affirm the Bible as a weapon in the struggle for liberation and claim that the God of the Bible is a God of the oppressed, feminist writers since the inauguration of the women's movement in the last century have maintained, to the contrary, that the Bible and Christian theology are inherently sexist and thereby destructive of women's consciousness. A revisionist interpretation of Scripture and theology, therefore, either will subvert women's struggle for liberation from all sexist oppression and violence, or will be forced to reinterpret Christian tradition and theology in such a way that nothing "Christian" will remain.

Feminist theology as a critical theology of liberation must defend itself on two sides: While liberation theologians are reluctant to acknowledge that women are exploited and oppressed, radical feminist thinkers claim that feminist consciousness and Christian faith are contradictions in terms. When our daughter Christina was born, we announced her baptism with the following statement:

> She is born into a world of oppression
> She is born into a society of discrimination
> She is reborn into a church of inequality. . .

The reaction of our friends to this announcement illustrates these objections to Christian feminist theology. Some colleagues and students in theology shook their heads and asked whether we had planned a Marxist initiation rite. Others in indignation pointed to the privileged status of a girl born to middle-class professional parents. A very bright college student (who felt suffocated by the patriarchal environment of the university and was later hospitalized with a nervous breakdown) challenged me on the street, saying, How can you do this to her? She will never be able to be a consciousness-raised woman and a committed Christian. Christian faith and the Church are destructive of women as persons who struggle against sexism for liberation.

The question feminist theologians must face squarely is thus a foundational theological problem: Is being a woman and being a Christian a primary contradiction that must be resolved in favor of one to the exclusion of the other? Or can both be kept in creative tension so that my being a Christian supports my struggle for liberation as a woman, and my being a feminist enhances and deepens my commitment to live as a Christian?[22] Since feminist theology as a Christian theology is bound to its charter documents in Scripture, it must formulate this problem with reference to the Bible and biblical revelation. Since the Bible was and is used against women's demand for equality and liberation from societal, cultural, and ecclesial sexism, it must conceive of this task first in critical terms before it can attempt to formulate a hermeneutics of liberation. While the danger of liberation theology is "proof texting," the pitfall to be avoided by feminist theology is apologetics, since such an apologetics does not take the political implications of scriptural interpretation seriously.

The debate surrounding *The Woman's Bible*, which first appeared in two volumes in 1895 and 1898, may serve as a case study for the *political* conditions and implications of feminist biblical interpretation as well as for the radical critical impact of feminist theology on the interpretive task.[23] In her introduction to *The Woman's Bible* Elizabeth Cady Stanton, the initiator of the project, outlined two critical insights for a feminist theological hermeneutics.

First, the Bible is not a "neutral" book; it is a political weapon against women's struggle for liberation. Second, this is so because the Bible bears the imprint of men who never saw or talked with God.

Elizabeth Cady Stanton conceived of biblical interpretation as a political act. The following episode characterizes her personal conviction of the negative impact of Christian religion on women's situation. She refused to attend a prayer meeting of suffragists that was opened by the singing of the hymn "Guide Us, O Thou Great Jehovah" by Isabella Beecher Hooker. Her reason was that Jehovah had "never taken any active part in the suffrage movement."[24] Because of her experience that Yahweh was not on the side of the oppressed, she realized the great political influence of the Bible. She therefore proposed to prepare a revision of the Bible that would collect and interpret (with the help of "higher criticism") all statements referring to women in the Bible. She conceded, however, that she was not very successful in soliciting the help of women scholars because they were

> afraid that their high reputation and scholarly attainments might be compromised by taking part in an enterprise that for a time may prove very unpopular. Hence we may not be able to get help from that class.[25]

And, indeed, the project of *The Woman's Bible* proved to be very unpopular because of political implications. Not only did some of the suffragists argue that such a project was either unnecessary or politically unwise, but the National American Woman's Suffrage Association formally rejected it as a political mistake. In the second volume, which appeared in 1898, Cady Stanton sums up this opposition by reporting, "Both friend and foe object to the title." She then replies with biting wit to the accusation of a clergyman that *The Woman's Bible* is "the work of women and the devil."

> This is a grave mistake. His Satanic Majesty was not to join the Revising Committee which consists of women alone. Moreover, he has been so busy of late years

attending Synods, General Assemblies and Conferences, to prevent the recognition of women delegates,
that he has no time to study the languages and "higher
criticism."[26]

Although the methods and theological presuppositions
of the "higher criticism" of the time are outdated today,
the political arguments and objectives of a feminist biblical
interpretation remain valid. They are outlined by Cady
Stanton in her introduction to the first volume. She gives
three reasons an objective scientific feminist revision and
interpretation of the Bible is politically necessary. First,
throughout history the Bible has been used to keep women
in subjection and to hinder their emancipation. Second,
not only men, but especially women are the most faithful
believers in the Bible as the Word of God; not only for
men, but also for women the Bible has a numinous authority. Third, no reform is possible in one area of society
if it is not advanced in all other areas. One cannot reform
the law and other cultural institutions without also reform-
ing biblical religion. Since "all reforms are interdependent," a critical feminist interpretation is a necessary
political endeavor, though perhaps not opportune. If feminists think they can neglect the revision of the Bible because there are more pressing political issues, then they do
not recognize the political impact of Scripture upon the
churches and society, and also upon the lives of women.

Cady Stanton advocated a revision of the Bible in terms
of "higher criticism," Her insights, therefore, correspond
with the results of historical biblical studies of her time. In
contrast to the doctrinal understanding of the Bible as the
Word of God, she stresses that the Bible is written by men
and reflects patriarchal male interests. "The only point in
which I differ from all ecclesiastical teaching is that I do
not believe that any man ever saw or talked with God."[27]
While the churches teach that degrading ideas about patriarchal injunctions against women come from God, Cady
Stanton maintains that all these degrading texts and ideas
came from the minds of men. By treating the Bible as a
human work and not as a fetish, and by denying divine
inspiration to the negative biblical statements about wom-

en, her committee has shown more reverence and respect for God, in her view, than does the clergy or the church. She concedes that some teachings of the Bible, such as the love commandment or the golden rule, are still valid today, and since the teachings and lessons of the Bible differ from each other, the Bible cannot be accepted or rejected as a whole. Therefore, every passage on women must be carefully analyzed and evaluated for its impact on the struggle for the liberation of women.

Although the idea of a Bible consisting only of the biblical texts on women must be rejected today on methodological grounds,[28] biblical scholarship on the whole has proven accurate her contention that the Bible must be studied as a human work, and that biblical interpretation is influenced by the theological mind-set and interests of the interpreter. Contemporary feminist interpreters, like some of Cady Stanton's suffragist friends, either reject biblical interpretation as a hopeless feminist endeavor because the Bible is totally sexist, or attempt to defend the Bible in the face of its radical feminist critics. In doing so they follow Frances Willard, who argued against the radical critique of *The Woman's Bible* that only the patriarchal contemporary interpretation, not the biblical message, preaches the subjugation of women.

> I think that men have read their own selfish theories into the book, that theologians have not in the past sufficiently recognized the progressive quality of its revelation nor adequately discriminated between its records as history and its principles of ethics and religion.[29]

The insight that scholarly biblical interpretations need to be "depatriarchalized" is an important one, but it should not be misunderstood as an apologetic defense of the nonpatriarchal character of the Bible's teachings on ethics and religion. Elizabeth Cady Stanton's point was that the Bible is not simply misunderstood; its contents and perspectives can be used in the political struggle against women. Gustavo Gutierrez's comments on human historiography in general are applicable to the writing of the Bible:

> Human history has been written by a white hand, a male hand from the dominating social class. The perspective of the defeated in history is different. Attempts have been made to wipe from their minds the memory of their struggles. This is to deprive them of a source of energy, of an historical will to rebellion.[30]

If we compare Cady Stanton's hermeneutical stance with that of Segundo, we see that she could not accept his understanding of a liberative second-level learning process within Christian history precisely because she shares his advocacy stance for the oppressed. Cady Stanton cannot begin with the affirmation that the Bible and the God of the Bible are on the side of the oppressed because her experience of the Bible as a political weapon against women's struggle for suffrage tells her otherwise.

The subsequent reaction to *The Woman's Bible* also warns liberation theologians that a biblical interpretation that resorts too quickly to the defense of the Bible could misconstrue its advocacy stance for the oppressed. The task of liberation theologians is not to prove that the Bible or the church can be defended against feminist or socialist attacks, but rather to critically comprehend how the Bible functions in the oppression of women or the poor and thus to prevent its misuse for further oppression. The advocacy stance of liberation theology can only be construed as a rationalization of preconceived ecclesiastical or dogmatic positions if it does not fully explore the oppressive aspects of biblical traditions. Because of their advocacy stance for the oppressed, feminist theologians must insist that theological-critical analysis of Christian tradition should not begin with the time of Constantine, but it should include the Christian charter documents.

Because of its allegiance to the "defeated in history," a feminist critical theology maintains that a hermeneutics of consent that understands itself as the "actualizing continuation of the Christian history of interpretation" does not suffice. This hermeneutics overlooks the fact that Christian Scripture and tradition are not only a source of truth but also of untruth, repression, and domination. Since the hermeneutic-contextual paradigm seeks only to understand biblical texts, it cannot adequately consider that the Christian past as well as its interpretations has victimized women. A critical theology of liberation, therefore, must develop a new interpretive paradigm that can take seriously the claim of liberation theologians that God is on the side of the oppressed.[31] The paradigm must also accept the claim of feminist theologians that God has never "taken an active part in the suffrage movement," and that therefore the Bible can function as a male weapon in the political struggle against women's liberation.

III. Toward a Feminist Interpretive Paradigm of Emancipatory Praxis[32]

A critical theology of liberation cannot avoid raising the question of the truth content of the Bible for Christians today. If, for instance, feminist theologians take fully into account the androcentric language, misogynist contents, and patriarchal interests of biblical texts, then we cannot avoid the question of the "canon," or the criterion that allows us to reject oppressive traditions and to detect liberating traditions within biblical texts and history.

The need for a critical evaluation of the various biblical texts and traditions has always been recognized by the church. While the doctrinal paradigm insisted that Scripture must be judged by the *regula fidei*, and can only be properly interpreted by the teaching office of the church, the historical-critical paradigm evaluated the theological truth of biblical texts according to their historicity. The hermeneutic-contextual paradigm has not only established the canon as the multiform root-model of the Christian community, but has also stressed that the Bible often includes various contradictory responses to the historical situation of the Israelite or Christian community.

Since not all these responses can equally express Christian revelation, biblical scholarship has attempted to formulate theological criteria to evaluate different biblical traditions. This "canon within the canon" can be formulated along philosophical-dogmatic or historical-factual lines. Some theologians distinguish between revelatory essence and historical expression, timeless truth and culturally conditioned language, or constant Christian tradition and changing traditions. When such a canon is formulated along the lines of the hermeneutic-contextual paradigm, scholars juxtapose Jesus and Paul, Pauline theology and early Catholicism, the historical Jesus and the kerygmatic Christ, or Hebrew and Greek thought. For example, Ogden accepts the Jesus traditions of Marxsen,[33] and Sobrino emphasizes the Jesus of history as the criterion for liberation theology. Segundo is methodologically most consistent when he insists that no contentual biblical statement can be singled out as a criterion because all historical expression of faith is ideological. In line with the hermeneutic-contextual paradigm, he insists that the process of interpretation within the Bible and Christian history, not the content, should be normative for liberation theology. Yet this position overlooks that the process of expressing faith in a historical situation can also be falsified and serve oppressive interests.

Therefore, a critical theology of liberation cannot take the Bible or the biblical faith defined as the total process of learning through ideologies as *norma normans non normata*, but must understand them as sources alongside other sources.[34] This point has been made by James Cone, who pointed out that the sources of theology are the Bible as well as our own political situation and experience; the norm for black theology is *"Jesus as the Black Christ who provides the necessary soul for black liberation . . . he is the essence of the Christian gospel."*[35]

I would be hesitant to postulate that Jesus as the feminist Christ is the canonical norm, since we cannot spell out concretely who this feminist Christ is if we do not want to make Christ a formalized cipher or resort to mysticism. This is the argument of Jon Sobrino, who postulates that the historical Jesus is the norm of truth, since *"access to the Christ of faith comes through our following of the historical Jesus."*[36] Yet such a formulation of the canonical norm for Christian faith presupposes that we can know the

historical Jesus and that we can imitate him, since an
actual following of Jesus is not possible for us. Moreover, a
feminist theologian must question whether the historical
man Jesus of Nazareth can be a role model for contemporary women, since feminist psychologists point out that
liberation means the struggle of women to free ourselves
from all internalized male norms and models.

I would suggest that the canon and norm for evaluating
biblical traditions and their subsequent interpretations
cannot be derived from the Bible or the biblical process of
learning within ideologies, but can only be formulated
within the struggle for the liberation of women and all oppressed people. The canon and evaluative norm cannot be
"universal," but must be specific and derived from a particular experience of oppression and liberation. The advocacy stance of liberation theologies must be sustained at
the point of the critical evaluation of biblical texts and
traditions. The personally and politically reflected experience of oppression and liberation must become the criterion of "appropriateness" for biblical interpretation.

A hermeneutical understanding that is oriented toward
an actualizing continuation of biblical history, as well as
toward a critical evaluation of it, must uncover and
denounce biblical traditions and theologies that perpetuate
violence, alienation, and oppression. At the same time, a
critical hermeneutics must also delineate those biblical
traditions that bring forward the liberating experiences and
visions of the people of God. Such a hermeneutics points
to the eschatological vision of freedom and salvation, and
maintains that such a vision must be historically realized
in the community of faith.

A feminist theological interpretation of the Bible that
has as its canon the liberation of women from oppressive
sexist structures, institutions, and internalized values must
maintain, therefore, that only the nonsexist and nonpartriar-
chal traditions of the Bible and the nonoppressive traditions of biblical interpretation have the theological authority of revelation if the Bible is not to continue as a tool for
the oppression of women. The advocacy stance demands
that oppressive and destructive biblical traditions not be
granted their claim to truth and authority today.[37] Nor did

they have a valid claim at any point in history. A critical hermeneutics must be applied to their subsequent history of interpretation in order to determine how much these traditions and interpretations have contributed to the patriarchal oppression of women. In the same vein, a critical feminist hermeneutics must rediscover those biblical traditions and interpretations that have transcended their oppressive cultural contexts even though they are embedded in patriarchal culture. These texts and traditions should not be understood as abstract theological ideas or norms, but as responses of faith to concrete historical situations of oppression. For instance, throughout the centuries Christian feminism has claimed Galatians 3:28 as its Magna Charta, whereas the patriarchal church has used 1 Corinthians 14 or 1 Timothy 2 for the cultural and ecclesiastical oppression of women.[38]

The insight that the Bible is not only a source of truth and revelation but also a source of violence and domination is basic for liberation theologies. This insight demands a new paradigm of biblical interpretation that does not understand the Bible as archetype but rather as prototype.

A dictionary definition reveals the significant distinction between the words. While both archetype and prototype "denote original models," an archetype is "usually construed as an ideal form that establishes an unchanging pattern." . . . However . . . a prototype is not a binding, timeless pattern, but one critically open to the possibility, even the necessity of its own transformation. Thinking in terms of prototypes historicizes myth.[39]

Since the hermeneutic-contextual paradigm seeks to appropriate biblical truth and history, but not its ideological critique, liberation theologians must develop a new critical paradigm of biblical interpretation. Thomas S. Kuhn has pointed out that a new scientific paradigm must also create a new scientific ethos and community.

The hermeneutic-contextual-historical paradigm accepts the advocacy stance within the hermeneutical circle as a presupposition from which to raise questions, but objects to it as a conviction or definite standpoint. A new critical paradigm must reject this as ideological. It must, in turn, insist that all theologians and interpreters of the Bible stand publicly accountable for their own positions. It should become methodologically *mandatory* for *all* scholars to state explicitly their own presuppositions, allegiances, and functions within a theological-political context, and especially for those scholars, who, in critique of liberation theology, resort to an artificially construed value-neutrality. Scholars no longer can pretend that what we do is completely "detached" from all political interests. Since we always interpret the Bible and Christian faith from a position within history, scholarly detachment and neutrality must be unmasked as a fiction or false consciousness that serves definite political interests. Further, theological interpretation must also critically reflect on the political presuppositions and implications of theological "classics" and doctrinal or ethical systems. In other words, we must scrutinize not only the content and "tradition-ing" process within the Bible but also the entire Christian tradition, and determine whether or not it serves to oppress or liberate people.

Finally, the advocacy stance as a criterion or norm for evaluating biblical texts and their political functions should not be mistaken for an abstract, formalized principle. The different expressions of liberation theology must construct specific heuristic models that adequately analyze the mechanisms and structures of contemporary oppression and movements for liberation. On the one hand, too generalized an understanding of oppression and liberation serves the interests of the oppressive system, which cannot tolerate a critical analysis of their dehumanizing mechanisms and structures. At the same time, it prevents the formulation of specific goals and strategies for the liberation struggle. On the other hand, too particularized an understanding of oppression and liberation prevents an active solidarity among oppressed groups, who can be played against each other by the established systems. The advocacy stance as the criterion or norm for biblical interpretation must develop, therefore, a critical theology of liberation that promotes the solidarity of all oppressed peoples, and at the same time has room enough to develop specific heuristic theological models of oppression and liberation.[40]

Liberation theologians must abandon the hermeneutic-contextual paradigm of biblical interpretation, and construct within the context of a critical theology of liberation a new interpretive paradigm that has as its aim emancipatory praxis. Such a paradigm of political praxis has, as a research perspective, the critical relationship between theory and practice, between biblical texts and contemporary liberation movements. This new paradigm of emancipatory praxis must generate new heuristic models that can interpret and evaluate biblical traditions and their political function in history in terms of their own canons of liberation.

4.

Discipleship and Patriarchy
Toward a Feminist Evaluative Hermeneutics

THE STUDIES OF ETHICS in the new Testament and its various themes and problems are vast, and the discussions on the use of the Bible in Christian moral theology are numerous.[1] To summarize the contents of the literature on biblical ethics and to discuss the theoretical-theological aspects adequately in a brief chapter would be presumptuous. To assume a relationship and interaction between Christian ethics and early Christian ethos, between contemporary moral theological reflection and first-century ethical instruction, is conventional but nevertheless poses difficulties. The hermeneutic-methodological problems raised by the encounter of a predominantly philosophical-systematic mode of inquiry with a historical-critical mode of analysis are complex and far from being resolved. Nevertheless there seems to be agreement among scholars that common ground for the two disciplines exists within the church, since the "community of Christian Scriptures" is also the "community of moral discourse." Not only do the Scriptures provide resources for the church's moral discourse and systematic reflection in Christian ethics, but they also form and guide the Christian community as a people "who derive their identity from a book."[2] The moral authority of the Bible is grounded in a community that is capable of sustaining Scriptural authority in faithful remembrance, liturgical celebration, ecclesial governance, and continual reinterpretation of its own biblical roots and traditions.

By locating the authority and significance of Scripture for Christian ethics in the community of faith,[3] we can positively assimilate the results of biblical scholarship,

which has for a long time stressed that the community of
Israel and of early Christianity is the *Sitz im Leben* of biblical writings. Biblical texts have to be read in their communal, social, and religious contexts and understood as
responses of faith to particular historical situations.[4] No
systematization of biblical moral injunctions, therefore,
seems possible. It is misleading to speak about a uniform
biblical or New Testament ethics, since the Bible is not
a book but a collection of literary texts that span almost
a millennium of history and culture. Although some simi-
larity in themes or in religious perspectives can be established, such a systematization depends on the selective
activity of the biblical interpreter, on the systematic construction of the ethicist, or on the one-sided selection of
the church rather than on the unilateral and clear-cut
authority of Scripture. Therefore neither the biblical nor
the moral theologian can eschew hermeneutical reflection
and critical evaluation of biblical traditions.

While the multiformity of biblical ethos and ethics has
long been recognized and the concomitant quest for the
"canon within the canon" is much debated in Biblical
scholarship,[5] the discussions among ethicists on the authority of the Bible and its use in moral discourse seem not
to center on the need for a critical *evaluative* hermeneutics[6] of the Bible and Christian tradition. Remembrance
can be nostalgic, and reinterpretation of oppressive traditions can serve to maintain the status quo. The history of
the church and its appeal to the authority of Scripture
shows that biblical traditions are not only life giving but
also death dealing. The appeal to Scripture has authorized,
for example, the persecution of Jews, the burning of
witches, the torture of heretics, national wars in Europe,
the subhuman conditions of American slavery, and the
antisocial politics of the Moral Majority.

The political appeal to the moral authority of the Bible
can be dangerous if it is sustained by the "community of
the forgiven" but not by the church always in need of reform. It can be especially dangerous if the Christian community is shaped by the remembrance of "the historical
winners" while abandoning the subversive memory of

innocent suffering and of solidarity with the victims of history.[7] In short, the Bible and its subsequent interpretations are sources for both liberation and oppression. As I have already emphasized, the Bible can be a resource for solving moral problems and generating moral challenges, as well as for legitimizing dehumanization and violence. The moral character of its theological vision and the moral injunctions of its traditions must be assessed and adjudicated in critical theological discourse if Scripture is to function as revelation "given for the sake of our salvation."[8]

It is obvious by now that this caveat shares in the moral impetus and theoretical insights of political and liberation theologies, which do not seek to use Scripture "as an ideology for justifying the demands of the oppressed."[9] Rather they strive to rescue the biblical vision of liberation from the ideological distortions of those who have formulated, interpreted, and used the Bible against the cultural and ecclesiastical victims of the past and the present.

From its inception feminist interpretation of and concern with Scripture have been generated by the fact that throughout Christian history the Bible has been used to halt the emancipation of slaves and of women, on the one hand, and to justify such emancipation, on the other hand. Elizabeth Cady Stanton spoke eloquently on the use of the Bible as a weapon against women's demand for political and ecclesial equility:

> From the inauguration of the movement for woman's emancipation the Bible has been used to hold her in the "divinely ordained sphere" prescribed in the Old Testament and New Testament. The canon and civil law, church and state, priests and legislators, all political parties and religious denominations have alike taught that woman was made after man, of man, an inferior being, subject to man. Creeds, codes, Scriptures and statutes are all based on this idea.[10]

As in the last century so also today the Bible is used against the women's liberation movement in society and church. Whenever women protest against political discrimination, economic exploitation, social inequality, and secondary status in the churches, the Bible is invoked because it teaches the divinely ordained subordination of women and the creational differences between the sexes. Anti-ERA groups, the cultural Total Woman Movement, and the Moral Majority appeal to the teachings of the Bible on the family and Christian womanhood. These right-wing political movements, which defend the American family in the name of biblical Christianity, do not hesitate to quote the Bible against shelters for battered women, for physical punishment of children, and against abortion, even in case of rape or teenage pregnancy.[11]

Yet throughout the centuries the Bible has not only served to justify theologically the oppression of slaves and women. It has also provided authorization for Christian women and men who rejected slavery and patriarchal subjection as un-Christian. This dialectical use of the Bible in the moral-theological discourse of the Church could be amply documented. A careful survey of the history of biblical interpretation would show that in the Church's moral discourse on women's role and dignity, certain key passages have emerged and had *formative* historical imimpact.[12] Key passages are Galatians 3:28, the appeal to the women prophets of the Old and New Testaments, and the gospel stories of Mary and Martha or of the Woman at the Well.

Key texts for the moral-theological justification of the patriarchal limitation and repression of women's leadership and roles include Genesis 2-3 and the prescriptive New Testament texts demanding the submission and silence of women in patriarchal marriage and church. No doubt, the church as the community of moral discourse is shaped by the scriptural trajectory of *Haustafeln* (household codes) and their faithful remembrance and reinterpretation. The church's dominant structures and articulations are patriarchal and until very recently its moral and theological leadership was exclusively male. The ongoing formative power of these biblical texts has led to the silencing or marginalization of women in the church and legitimized our societal and ecclesiastical exploitation by patriarchal family and church structures. In contemporary democratic society the Bible and biblical religion often serve to strengthen politically antidemocratic elements by reproducing ancient patriarchal structures of inequality and slavelike conditions in the family and the economy. The political alliance of anti-ERA and antiabortion forces with conservative biblical religion becomes understandable in light of these scriptural texts.

At this point the objection could be raised that such an assessment of the "politics and ethics of biblical remembrance" not only seriously misconstrues the church's moral discourse on Scripture but also overestimates the political function of the Bible as a dated historical-cultural formation. Yet the political strength of such right-wing movements as the Moral Majority documents how certain biblical remembrances can be employed successfully in the contemporary political struggle. This continuing cultural-political influence of the Bible has been, in my opinion, largely overlooked by many in the contemporary feminist movement, who have written off both organized religion and traditional family rather than identifying specific patrirachal structures and elements *within* biblical religion and family. This wholesale rejection of religion has played into the hands of the present conservative elements.

Finally, the contention that the political right and Christian feminists equally misuse the Bible for their own purposes requires a scholarly historical and theological assessment of the specific texts cited in the contemporary political struggle. In other words, public discussion needs to move from generalized moral and political discourse in church and society to disciplined theological scholarship if we are to assess the *political* function of biblical remembrance, that is, if we are to judge the impact of biblical traditions and texts on the contemporary Christian community and on American culture, which is still largely, if superficially, shaped by biblical religion. Accordingly, I propose here a development of biblical ethics that does not presuppose the apolitical character of Scripture and assume that *all* biblical tradition and texts have the authority of Scripture and promote the "common good" merely by reason of their inclusion in the canon.

I do not assume that in such a disciplined discourse the biblical exegete will provide only the historical-cultural "data" for systematic reflection and moral-theological evaluation, since such a division of labor would neglect the insights of the hermeneutical discussion itself. Instead I envision a disciplined dialogue between biblical scholars and moral theologians that enhances the critical-reflective competence of the whole Christian community. To this end I will first sketch the historical-critical assessment of one New Testament ethical tradition and its theological significance and meaning for today as asserted by biblical scholars. Then I will evaluate their biblical theological interpretations from a feminist perspective and discuss the elements of a feminist critical *evaluative* hermeneutics.

Because of the contemporary political discussion the so-called New Testament household codes and their scholarly interpretation suggest themselves as a test case. My critical exploration of the household code trajectory and its discussion in contemporary exegetical scholarship is meant, therefore, as an invitation to others to investigate methodologically the same biblical tradition from the scholarly perspective and with the theoretical tools of Christian ethics. The purpose is to develop biblical ethics as an "evaluative hermeneutics" of biblical traditions and of the Christian communities they have shaped and are still shaping.

I. Historical-Critical Analyses of the Household Code

Scholars of early Christianity have already begun a critical-historical discussion and theological evaluation of the household code trajectory, although they have not explicitly acknowledged its political dimensions. It is significant that scholarly interest in and investigation of these texts increased in the past decade, the same time when the women's movement in the churches developed momentum and urgency. The most recent works of Balch,[13] Clark,[14] and Elliott[15] testify to this growing scholarly interest, whereas those of Niederwimmer,[16] Crouch,[17] and Thraede[18] mark the beginning of this period. During the same time works on women in the Bible also have proliferated. Whereas these works usually concede or make explicit their inspiration by the women's movement, academic studies generally profess their allegiance to the so-called disinterested neutral paradigm of historical-critical scholarship. They therefore reject as unscientific any suggestion that they also might be determined by questions of contemporary relevance and political commitment. Yet a critical review of historical interpretations and theological-hermeneutic justifications of the household code ethic can illustrate the hermeneutical dependence of scholarly interests and historical evaluations on their contemporary social situations.

The texts classified as household code—a label derived from Lutheran teaching on social status and roles (Ständelehre)—are concerned with three sets of relationships: wife and husband, slave and master, and father and son. Each pair receives reciprocal admonitions. The central interest of these texts lies in the enforcement of the submission and obedience of the socially weaker group—wives, slaves, and children—on the one hand, and in the authority of the head of the household, the *pater familias*, on the other hand.

The complete form of the household code is only found in Colossians 3:18-4:1 and Ephesians 5:22-6:9. It is not found in the remaining passages: 1 Peter 2:18-3:7; 1 Timothy 2:11-15; 5:3-8; 6:1-2; Titus 2:2-10; 3:1-2; 1 Clement 21:6-8; Ignatius to Polykarp 4:1-6:2; Polykarp 4:2-6:1; Didache 4:9-11; Barnabas 19:5-7. One must therefore ask whether the three pairs of reciprocal relationships found only in Colossians and Ephesians are characteristic of the form, or whether the pattern of submissiveness is the most significant element.[19] The pattern of subjection need not always include all six social status groups addressed in Colossians and Ephesians. The pattern sometimes mentions only some of the subordinate groups, or it can include obedience to the political powers of the state or address the governance of the Christian community. The injunction to submissiveness occurs already in the authentic Pauline letters, for example, in Romans 13 and 1 Corinthians 14. It therefore cannot be attributed solely to what exegetes call early Catholicism.[20] While this pattern of submissiveness functions differently in different early Christian documents and their social-ecclesial-historical contexts, the "household dimension"[21] seems characteristic. This trajectory conceives not only of family but also of church and state in terms of the patriarchal household. The Christian community soon comes to be called "the household of God," and from the time of Augustus the Roman emperor is understood as the *pater patriae.*[22]

Much of the discussion of the household codes has focused on their historical-religious background, as well as on their theological meaning and authority or their "Christian" character. More recent research has raised significant questions as to their philosophical provenance and their social function, especially in view of emancipatory tendencies in the first century.

Philosophical Provenance

Recent discussions seem to have made a significant breakthrough regarding the philosophical provenance of the code. Although some exegetes maintained that the household code was uniquely Christian[23] because it addressed the subordinate group as moral agents, for some time the majority of scholars believed that the household code was patterned after the Stoic code of duty[24] and was probably mediated by Hellenistic Jewish propaganda. Now this scholarly consensus seems to give way to another interpretation. This new interpretation does not exclude the parallel of the Stoics and has the added virtue of accounting for the three pairs of subordinate relationships and reciprocal admonitions.

Independently of each other, the classicist Thraede and the New Testament scholars Lührmann, Balch, and Elliott have concluded that the household code texts share in the Aristotelian philosophical trajectory concerning household management (*oikonomia*) and political ethics (*politeia*). If this is the case, a political, philosophical tradition quite different from the Stoic code of duties is present, one concerned with the relationships between rulers and ruled in household and state. Here the patriarchal household is the point of reference and the household codes would better be named, in my opinion, "patterns of patriarchal submission."

Exegetes have long recognized that the household code trajectory christianizes patriarchal social and ecclesial structures. Thus recent research has clarified the philosophical-political underpinnings of this pattern. Aristotle, in contrast to the Sophists, stressed that the patriarchal relationships in household and city, as well as their concomitant social differences, are based not on social convention but on "nature." He therefore insisted that the discussion of political ethics and household management begin with marriage, defined as the union of natural ruler and natural subject (Politeia I. 1252a. 24–28). Balch's research documents a growing interest among diverse philosophical directions and schools in the first century to reassert this Aristotelian political ethos, albeit often in a modified, milder form.[25]

The household code ethic of the New Testament shares in this stabilizing reception of Aristotelian ethics and politics. The studies of the social world of early Christianity, recognizing the significant role of the house-church for the early Christian mission, suggest that the patriarchal ethics of the household expresses the ethos of the early Christian mission. G. Theissen, for example, proposes that the radical ethos of the Jesus movement was afamilial and ascetic, whereas the communities of the Christian missionary movement in the upcoming Greco-Roman urban centers were characterized by a softened form of patriarchalism, which with Troeltsch he terms *Liebespatriarchalismus.*[26]

J. H. Elliott follows this line of argument and seeks to show that the ethical instructions for the household in 1 Peter derive their significance from their connection with the early Christian missionary community as the "household of God." He elaborates the function and significance of the household for Greco-Roman politics and in the traditions of the Old and New Testaments. He concludes his survey with this observation:

Historically the *oikos* was the fundamental social locus and focus of the Christian movement. . . . It was not merely individuals but entire households who were converted and transformed by the good news of human reconciliations and of the new possibilities of life in the community. . . . As a socially revered institution with honorable goals and values, this extended Christian family posed no necessary threat to existing political institutions. To the contrary, focus on the familial nature and character of the Christian community enabled the movement to accentuate precisely those virtues of social life which were held in respect by society as a whole.[27]

Elliott's line of argument is based on the unproven assumption that the house-church was structured in keeping with the ethics of the household code and represented a Christian form of the patriarchal household. This assumption overlooks the fact that the house-church was not congruent with the existing household, since the conversion of entire households was not the norm in early Christianity. Indeed, the Christian missionary movement conflicted with the existing order of the patriarchal household because it converted *individuals* independently of their social status and function in the patriarchal household. Christian mission caused social unrest because it admitted wives and slaves as well as daughters and sons into the house-church, even when the *pater familias* was still pagan and had not converted to Christianity. The pagan accusation that Christian mission was subversive and destroyed patriarchal household structures was still being made in the second century. This accusation was not a misunderstanding or slander but an accurate perception of the social implications of conversion to Christianity. The household code ethics is an attempt to mitigate the subversive impact of religious conversion on the patriarchal order of the house and of society.

Social Function

The social implications of religious conversion were realized in the house-church as the discipleship community of equals. Independently of their fathers and husbands, women held membership and gained leadership positions in the Christian missionary movement.[28] Even in the beginning of the second century female and male slaves still expected their freedom to be purchased by the Christian community, as the letters of Ignatius and the Shepherd of Hermas document. Paul's letter to Philemon, the only New Testament writing addressed to a house-church, mentions a woman among the leadership of the church in Philemon's house. (Later exegetes understood her to be Philemon's wife though she is not so designated by Paul.) In this letter Paul insists with all the means of ancient rhetoric that Onesimus must be accepted into the house-church as a "beloved sibling," both as a Christian and as a human being.[29]

According to Mark's Gospel, the discipleship of equals is the community of brothers and sisters who do not have a "father." It is the "new family" that has replaced all the natural, social kinship ties of the patriarchal family. It does not consist of rulers and subjects, of relationships of super-ordination and subordination. According to Paul it is the *ekklesia*, the "assembly of the saints" who have equal access to God in the Spirit and are therefore coequal members in the body of Christ. Social roles in this *ekklesia* are not based on natural or social differences but on charismatic giftedness.

Sociologist R. Nisbet seems to have captured this ethos of the house-church better than some exegetes and theologians. He stresses the profoundly communal character of early Christianity and maintains that conflict was "the very essence of Christianity's relation to its age." This conflict was a conflict of values and of allegiances between the Christian community and the Roman patriarchal family.

Christianity like all evangelizing religions addressed its message to individuals—men, women, and children. And so long as the family remained an intact structure, just so long did its very structure act to mediate, even to interfere with the proselytizing efforts of the missionaries of Christ. The strategy from the Christian point of view was thus a vital and almost obvious one:

to denigrate so far as possible the historic and still deeply rooted kinship tie and offer the community of Christians itself as the only real and true form of kinship.[30]

Nisbet points to the emancipatory implications of such an ecclesial self-understanding for women. By offering the community as the new kinship structure, the Christian movement disengaged women from their traditional patriarchal family roles and limitations.

A statement by the classicist E. A. Judge would seem to contradict this observation, but when understood as referring to the household code ethics rather than to all New Testament writings, it makes the same point.

> With regard to the household obligation, the NT writers are unanimous; its bonds and conventions must at all costs be maintained . . . . There is of course . . . the interest of the patronal class . . . but the primary reason no doubt is that the entrenched rights of the household as a religious and social unit offered the Christians the best possible security for their existence as a group. Any weakening here would thus be a potentially devastating blow to their own cohesion, as well as having revolutionary implications from the point of view of the public authorities.[31]

Nevertheless Judge seems to think that the house-church was governed by the "principles of fraternity" and that it presented a threat only "if enthusiastic members failed to contain their principles within the privacy of the association and thus were led into political indiscretions or offences against the hierarchy of the household."[32] Such an argument overlooks that the conversion of women, slaves, and young people who belonged to the household of an unconverted *pater familias* already constituted a potential political offense against the patriarchal order. It had to be considered an infringement of the political order, for the patriarchal order of the house was considered the paradigm for the state. Since the patriarchal *familia* was the nucleus of the state, conversion of the subordinated members of the house who were supposed to share in the religion of the *pater familias* constituted a subversive act.

The prescriptive household code trajectory attempted to ameliorate this subversion by asserting the congruence of the Christian ethics with that of patriarchal house and state. This trajectory did not continue the ethos of the house-church, with its voluntary and collegial structures, but sought to modify it and bring it into line with the structures of patriarchal family and society.[33] In doing so the household code trajectory sought to patriarchalize not only the early Christian ethos of "fraternity," or more precisely of the discipleship of equals, but also the structures of the Christian community. However, the prescriptive character of these texts indicates that such a process of patriarchalization had not been accomplished by the beginning of the second century.

Emancipatory Tendencies in the First Century

While the household code trajectory appealed to the dominant patriarchal ethos of Greco-Roman society, the ethos of coequal discipleship appealed to the more egalitarian aspirations of Roman society.[34] This ethos was threatening precisely because it shared the general economic development and cultural mood that allowed for the greater freedom and independence of women from patriarchal control. K. Thraede has chided New Testament scholars for theologically misconstruing the meaning inherent in the household code trajectory because they do not take into account the lively public discussion on the "nature" and role of women in the first century.[35] Since the economic independence and the civil emancipation of women, especially wealthy women, had increased, the *patria potestas* often amounted to little more than a legal fiction. Moreover, Augustan legislation, while professing to strengthen the traditional patriarchal family, actually undermined it, insofar as the emperor increasingly usurped the powers of the *pater familias*.

Most of the literary statements and philosophical reflections on the nature and role of women are ruminations and prescriptions of educated men. They must be understood as arguments seeking to deal with a more emancipative social situation. On the one hand there are those who nostalgically conjure up the patriarchal beginnings of Rome and the impeccable behavior of Roman ancestral matrons, in order to demand the strict exercise of the *patria potestas*. On the other hand are those who stress the equality of women with men in nature, education, and social standing, although they do not usually go so far as to advocate complete equality of social role.

Thus, the reactivation of the Aristotelian ethos that maintains the social differences as *natural* differences between women and men, as well as between slaves and freeborn, has to be seen within the context of this cultural-political debate. In this context, the household code trajectory is seen not only to christianize this partriarchal Aristotelian ethics of inequality but also to humanize and modify it, by obliging the *pater familias* to exercise love, consideration, and responsibility. From the perspective of women and slaves, however, the household code ethos is a serious setback, since it does not strengthen Roman cultural tendencies to equality and mutuality between women and men.

By reinforcing the patriarchal submission of those who, according to Aristotle, must be ruled, the early Christian ethos of coequal discipleship loses its capacity to structurally transform the patriarchal order of family and state. And by adapting the Christian community to its patriarchal society, the household code ethos opens up the community to political co-optation by the Roman empire. That such a process of co-optation required centuries to complete speaks for the vitality of the early Christian ethos of coequal discipleship. In this process, nevertheless, the vision of *agape* and service, mutuality, and solidarity among Christians gradually becomes reduced from a "new reality" merely to a moral appeal. Submission and obedience, but not equality and justice, are institutionalized by the patriarchal ethos. Since this ethos was not restricted to the household but also adopted by the house-church, Christian faith and praxis ceased to provide a structural-political alternative to the dominant patriarchal culture. The church's preaching of the gospel and its hierarchical-patriarchal structures became a contradiction that robbed the gospel of its transforming power in history.

II. Biblical Theological Evaluation of the Household Code Ethics

Biblical interpretation always entails theological assessment and justification. So it remains to discuss the types of contemporary theological evaluations that are proposed as justification for the *Christian* character of this early Christian pattern of patriarchal submission. Three distinct lines of argument have emerged: necessary adaptation, goodness of creation, and subversive subordination.

Necessary Adaptation

In order to survive in a patriarchal culture, the church had to adapt its ethos and structures to the patriarchy of Greco-Roman society. Whenever this adaptation is viewed negatively, it is pointed out that the household codes belong only to the later New Testament and apostolic writings, and are not found in the genuine Pauline letters. Therefore they are a deformation of the early Christian ethos and of the Pauline gospel and must be understood as the outcome of early Catholicism. The adaptation of the gospel to its bourgeois society is usually ascribed to the disappearance of imminent eschatologial expectations.[36]

Other supporters of this line of argument point out that the household codes strenghtened the "cohesiveness" of the Christian group and provided institutional patterns that enabled the church to survive.[37] Whereas the Jesus movement was a conflict movement, the early Christian missionary movement was integrative because of its ethos of love-patriarchalism. The process of ecclesial "patriarchilization" was, in this view, part of the historically necessary development from charisma to office, from Paulinism to early Catholicism, from a millennarian radical ethos to a privileged Christian establishment, from the egalitarian structures of the beginnings to the hierarchical order of the Constantinian church.

This sociological-historical justification maintains that the patriarchalization of the early Christian movement was necessary if Christian communities were to grow, develop, and become historically viable. The institutionalization of the egalitarian Christian movement had to adopt patriarchal institutional structures. This theological justification, however, overlooks the fact that the house-church presents an *institutional* structure, which was patterned after the collegia rather than the patriarchal household. The household code would not have been formulated if other Christian institutional options had not already existed. By arguing for the necessity of the patriarchal character of the church as an institution, this sociological-historical justification implicitly maintains that the *institutional* church is inherently patriarchal and therefore must exclude the institutional leadership of women.

The Goodness of Creation

A second line of argument is especially attractive to German Lutherans. Supporters of this position argue that the household codes had a positive theological function by preventing the emigration of early Christians from "the world." The injunctions of the New Testament household codes affirm the goodness of creation, even though the later texts of the trajectory exhibit the inherent oppressive tendencies of the patriarchal pattern of submission. According to this line of argument the household codes are a social alternative to an unwordly, ascetic ethos that engendered flight from the world and withdrawal from society and cultured life. The ethics of the household code sustains the "worldliness of the New Testament," pronounces an energetic yes to the goodness of creation, and affirms marriage and family. In the household code ethics the order of creation, of marriage, family, and work, is accepted but not cosmologically justified and idealized. Instead this Christian ethics "is subordinated to the command of the Lord and especially oriented toward the well-being of the other."[38] The linking of the ethics of the household code to the command of the *Kyrios* enables Christians to live critically in the preordained structures of society.[39] In a similar fashion W. Schrage asserts:

To this Lord—so the *Haustafeln* stress—we owe obedience, not in a ghettolike sphere separated from the world, into which we retreat in ascetic flight from the world, not in a pure inwardness or an ecclesiastical territory, but in the societal-social domain. . . . As husbands and wives, as fathers and children, as masters and slaves, Christians must preserve their "new obedience" although social structures are thereby neither Christianized nor expected to be salvific. Certainly, the social formations are not obstructed, but they are also not sanctioned as rigid institutions.[40]

Thraede has aptly characterized such a panegyric of the household code ethics as so much theological *eisegesis*. And in spite of his own theological justification, E. Schweizer has conceded that the dynamics of the household code trajectory tends to preserve the freedom and social privilege of the *adult, free, male* Christian and to ensure the subjection of the socially weaker partner on Christian terms. In later texts the care for the partner, especially the socially weaker partner, recedes more and more into the background, even when love of neighbor is never completely forgotten. This theological evaluation of the household code texts therefore not only asserts the androcentric character of Christian ethics but ascribes the goodness of the world, marriage, and creation to oppressive patriarchal, societal, and ecclesial structures.

Subversive Subordination
The third line of apologetic argument also seeks to justify the household code's patriarchal ethics on theological grounds. Supporters of this position claim that the ethos of Jesus is expressed in the household codes because they reinforce Jesus' call to service. The codes therefore advocate an ethics of "revolutionary subordination." This "subordination means the acceptance of an *order* as it exists, but with the new meaning given to it by the fact that one's acceptance of its is willing and meaningfully motivated."[41] This assertion mistakenly presupposes that Greco-Roman ethics did not address the role of subordinate persons in the social and moral order. It also forgets that Jesus' call

to service in the gospels is addressed to those in power, to those who are first in the community, *not* to those who are least. It is addressed to "friends" and not to subordinates. Therefore, this call functions, not as a religious motivation for maintaining the existing patriarchal *Herrschaftsverhältnisse* in society and church, but for fostering the praxis of the early Christian ethos of coequality in discipleship. This equality is conceded in this line of argument, but only in the *religious*, personal, individual sphere.

> But if we are to understand the point of this passage [1 Cor. 11:2–16] we must assume that the women *had* heard that message. Otherwise, they would not be taking off their veils, especially not during the worship services. Thus the retention of the veil when a woman would rise to speak in the congregation . . . also became a symbol of that double movement: first of the enfranchising impact of the gospel upon woman in that she may rise to speak and can function *religiously* as far more than simply a member of the household of her father or husband, and secondly of her acceptance of the order of society within which her role is to be lived out. Here again as in the *Haustafeln* there is a clear reminder that this relationship of subordination and superordination is not a difference in worth. . . . To accept subordination within the framework of things *as they are* is not to grant the inferiority in moral or personal value of the subordinate party [emphasis added].[42]

One is surprised to find such an advocacy of "things as they are" formulated in a work that seeks to recapture those social dimensions of the biblical vision of reality "which stand in creative tension with the cultural functions of our age and perhaps any age." Yet this insistence on subordination becomes understandable when one observes that the dominant structures of our culture and society are understood as being determined by "sweeping egalitarianism." In this critique of K. Stendahl, J. H. Yoder asks: "What if, for instance, the sweeping, doctrinaire egalitarianism of our culture, which makes the concept of the 'place of women' seem either laughable or boorish, and makes that of 'subordination' seem insulting should turn out really (in the 'intent of God,' or in the long run of social experience) to be demonic, uncharitable, destructive of personality, disrespectful of creation, and unworkable?"[43] Thus Yoder defends the New Testament pattern of patriarchal submission because it motivates Christian slaves and women to accept "things as they are." He maintains that we must advocate it today because its injunctions are out of step with contemporary convictions "present ever since the age of Lincoln but propagated still more sweepingly with the currency of civil rights and women's liberation rhetoric." Yet a careful analysis of American economic-political realities could have shown that in contemporary society "egalitarianism" does not determine sociopolitical institutions and economic policies. Reaganite politics testifies to this.

All three attempts to explicate the ethics and ethos expressed in the household code trajectory are prepared to justify on theological grounds the historical and contemporary discrimination and oppression of those whose "nature" predisposes them to be "ruled" in patriarchal structures. The sociological-theological justification argues that the continuing existence and historical power of the institutional church legitimizes such patriarchal structures; the predominantly Lutheran justification maintains the goodness of the "world" and creation as concomitant with patriarchal structures; and the social-ethical approach of Barthian theology legitimizes the pattern of patriarchal submission as religious motivation for accepting the status quo of patriarchal social structures. All three arguments affirm the patriarchal character of biblical revelation and of the Christian church as well as document the ideological function of biblical theology and ethics. They support the postbiblical feminist claim that Christian theology and the Church are inherently sexist.

III. A Feminist Evaluative Hermeneutics of the Bible

Postbiblical feminists argue that biblical religion is not retrievable for feminists who are committed to the liberation of women. Biblical religion ignores women's experience, speaks of God in male language, and sustains women's positions of powerlessness by legitimizing women's societal and ecclesial subordination as well as male dominance and violence against women, especially against those caught in patriarchal marriage relationships. Therefore, it is argued, feminists must abandon biblical religion and reject the authority of the Bible. Revisionist interpretations are at best a waste of time and at worst a further legitimization of the prevailing sexism of biblical religion. Feminist vision and praxis must be rooted in the contemporary experience of women and cannot seek to derive legitimacy from the Christian past and the Bible.

Although this feminist critique of biblical religion must be taken seriously, it must also be pointed out that such a feminist strategy is in danger of too quickly conceding that women have no authentic history within biblical religion. It therefore too easily relinquishes women's feminist biblical heritage. Yet Western feminists cannot afford to deny our biblical heritage if we do not want to strengthen the powers of oppression that deprive people of their own history and contribute to the reality constructions of androcentric texts. Moreover this feminist strategy cannot sustain solidarity with and commitment to *all* women whether they are "liberated" or not.[44] It cannot respect the positive self-identity and vision that women still derive from biblical religion. Postbiblical feminism must either neglect the positive biblical influences on contemporary women or declare women's involvement with biblical religion a "false consciousness." However any social and cultural feminist transformation in Western society must deal constructively with biblical religion and its continuing impact on American culture. American women are not able to completely discard and forget our personal, cultural, and religious history. We will either transform biblical history and religion into a new liberating force or continue to be subject to its patriarchal tyranny. Feminist Christian theologians have responded in different ways to the challenge of post-Christian feminism and have sought to develop different hermeneutical frameworks for spelling out theologically what it means to be a self-identified woman and a Christian. We have developed therefore, different approaches to the interpretation and evaluation of biblical religion in general and biblical texts in particular. In my own work I have attempted to formulate a feminist Christian theology as a "critical theology of liberation."[45] I have done so with reference to contemporary oppression of women in society and church, especially my own church, as well as with respect to the Bible and early Christian history.

In the context of such a feminist theology I have sought to develop a feminist biblical hermeneutics as a critical evaluative hermeneutics.[46] This hermeneutics not only challenges androcentric constructions of biblical history in language but also critically analyzes androcentric texts in order, first, to arrive at the lived ethos of early Christians that developed in interaction with its patriarchal cultural contexts and, second, to critically determine and evaluate its continuing structures of alienation and liberation. This evaluative feminist hermeneutics uses the critical analytical methods of historical biblical scholarship on the one hand and the theological goals of liberation theologies on the other, but focuses on the historical struggles of women in patriarchal culture and religion.

Historical-critical scholarship has worked out the pluralism of the biblical experience of faith, ethos, and community. It has shown that biblical texts are embedded in the historical experiences of biblical people and that the Bible must be understood in the context of believing communities. It is therefore necessary to reconstruct as carefully as possible not only the structure of biblical texts but also the paradigms of biblical faith and communities shaped by experiences of faith. This interpretive paradigm of historical-critical scholarship often undertands the Bible as the prime model of Christian faith and community of faith.

A feminist critical hermeneutics of liberation seeks to read the Bible in the context of believing communities of women, of the "church of women." It realizes that a feminist re-vision and transformation of biblical history and community can only be achieved through a critical evaluation of patriarchal biblical history and androcentric texts. It recognizes, as a hermeneutic feminist principle, that being woman and being Christian is a social, historical, and cultural ecclesial process. What it means to be a Christian woman is not defined by essential female nature or timeless biblical revelation, but grows out of the concrete social structures and cultural-religious mechanisms of women's oppression as well as our struggles for liberation, selfhood, and transcendence. Feminist identity is not based on the perception of women defined by female biology or feminine gender and societal-ecclesial roles, but on the common historical experience of women as an oppressed people,[47] collaborating with our oppression and at the same time struggling for our liberation in patriarchal biblical history and community. A feminist critical hermeneutics of the household code texts has the aim, therefore, to become a "dangerous memory" that reclaims our foremothers' and foresisters' sufferings and struggles through the subversive power of the critically remembered past.

Such a critical feminist hermeneutics is distinct from a feminist hermeneutics that derives the "canon" of feminist Christian faith and ethos from the Bible and therefore isolates the "liberating" impulse of biblical vision from its oppressive aspects. Such a hermeneutics therefore seeks to distinguish between historically limited patriarchal traditions and the liberating biblical tradition,[48] between the liberating essence of the revealed text[49] and its historical patriarchal-cultural expression, between the liberating prophetic critique[50] and the Bible's historical-cultural deformations. Such a feminist hermeneutics seems sometimes more concerned with establishing the revelatory authority of certain biblical texts or traditions than with carefully analyzing the particular roots and historical structures of women's oppression and struggles for liberation in patriarchal biblical history and religion. Such a hermeneutics is, as a result, in danger of formulating a feminist biblical apologetics instead of sufficiently acknowledging and exploring the oppressive function of patriarchal biblical texts in the past and in the present. It would be a serious and fatal mistake to relegate the household code trajectory, for example, to culturally conditioned biblical traditions no longer valid today and thereby to overlook the authoritative-oppressive impact these texts still have in the lives of Christian women.

A feminist "politics and ethics of scriptural remembrance" that shapes the Christian community as a community of moral discourse must keep alive the sufferings and hopes of biblical women and other "subordinate" peoples[51] in order to change and transform the patriarchal structures and ideologies of the Christian churches shaped by the New Testament pattern of patriarchal submission and silence. In the final analysis a critical feminist hermeneutics of the Bible must call patriarchal biblical religion to personal and structural conversion of feminist praxis before it can proclaim that the communities shaped by the Scriptures are "the community of the forgiven." In the last analysis such an evaluative hermeneutics of liberation is geared not only to the liberation of women but also to the emancipation of biblical religion from patriarchal structures and ideologies so that the "gospel" can again be recognized as "the power of God for salvation" (Romans 1:16).

The critical evaluation of the household code trajectory and its scholarly interpretations has found that its patriarchal ethics was asserted in contrast to an "egalitarian" Christian ethos. Biblical and moral theologians have labeled this ethos as unrealistic enthusiasm, gnostic spiritualism, ascetic emigration, or antinomian behavior that did not take seriously the given patriarchal structures of the everyday life and world. Early Christian women and slaves who took the gospel of freedom seriously are thereby disqualified and their experience of faith and praxis are rendered rationally or theologically suspect. This preference for the historical feasibility and theological orthodoxy of the biblical pattern of patriarchal submission in contrast to the "unwordliness" or "heresy" of the egalitarian ethos implies a historical-theological evaluation that is not derived from the New Testament itself. Yet such an evaluative interpretation acknowledges that the New Testament testifies to an early Christian ethos of coequal discipleship. Otherwise scholars could not disparage it.

A feminist critical hermeneutics that derives its canon from the struggle of women and other oppressed peoples for liberation from patriarchal structures must, therefore, call scholarly interpretations and evaluations to account and must carefully analyze their theological-political presuppositions and social-ecclesial interests. By making explicit its own evaluative feminist canons of liberation, this hermeneutics can reclaim the early Christian ethos of the discipleship of equals as its own biblical roots and heritage. In doing so it engenders a paradigm shift in biblical ethics insofar as it does not appeal to the Bible as its primary source but begins with women's own experience and vision of liberation.

In this feminist evaluative paradigm the Bible and biblical revelation no longer function as a timeless archetype but as a historical prototype open to feminist theological transformation.[52] The Bible is not the controlling and defining "court of appeals" for contemporary biblical feminist theology and community but its *formative* root-model. Only when viewed in this way can biblical revelation be liberated from its imprisonment in androcentric language and cultural-historical patriarchy. Only through a critical evaluative process of feminist hermeneutics can Scripture be used as a resource in the liberation struggle of women and other "subordinated" people. The vision and praxis of our foresisters who heard the call to coequal discipleship and acted in the power of the Spirit must be allowed to become a transformative power that can open up a feminist future for biblical religion.

A feminist biblical future depends on both the faithful remembrance of the oppression and liberation of women in biblical history and the critical exploration of the continuing effects of the household code trajectory in our own time and democratic society. A feminist evaluative exploration is rooted in the personal experience of women and utilizes feminist scholarship and scientific theoretical discussion. While feminist theology has severely criticized and challenged present-day patriarchal church structures, it has not sufficiently utilized the theoretical feminist critique of marriage and family as the place of women's patriarchal oppression. It has concentrated on the analysis of cultural dualisms, but not sufficiently explored their ideological roots in patriarchal societal structures.

Susan Moller Okin, a political philosopher, has shown that the Aristotelian political ethics of the household code still operates in contemporary American democratic society. Although the patriarchal family has been modified in the course of history, political philosophy still accepts the Aristotelian premise that the free, propertied man is the full citizen, whereas

> all the other members of the population—slaves and artisans as well as women—exist in order to perform their respective function for the few free males who participate fully in citizenship. The "natures" of all these groups of people are defined in terms of their sastifactory performance of their conventional functions.[53]

For the Greeks the private, secluded sphere of the household was important primarily as an economic base, whereas in modern times it is also crucial as a highly important aspect of affective life. Since the wife is responsible for the private sphere of the household, even a liberal philosopher such as John Stuart Mill asserts that she can only take on outside responsibilities after she has successfully taken care of *her* domestic ones.

Even though liberalism is supposed to be based on individualism and to understand society as constituted of "independent, autonomous units," it is clear, according to Moller Okin, that in spite of this individualistic rhetoric, the "family" and not the adult human individual is the basic political unit of liberal and nonliberal philosophers. The adult members of family are assumed to share all the same interests. Yet whenever a conflict of interest occurs between husband and wife, the presumption in political and legal philosophy has been that a conflict of interest must be decided by the male head of the household. More-

over, the public political sphere of "man's world" is
defined by competition and self-interest, not by values of
compassion, love, and altruism, since such values are
relegated to the private sphere of the home as women's domain. To legally and politically recognize women as individual citizens in their own right would entail, therefore, a
change in the family structure and political philosophy.
Moller Okin concludes:

> If our aim is a truly democratic society, or a thorough-
> ly democratic theory, we must acknowledge that any-
> thing but a democratic family with complete equality
> and mutual interdependence between the sexes will be
> a severe impediment to this aim.[54]

She also points out that the radical feminist critique of
marriage and family must be specified as both a critique of
patriarchal household and societal relationships and an
affirmation of interpersonal relationships of adult members who live in a "familial" community. Moreover, feminists have to recognize that woman's oppression is not the
result of her biological endowments but of her function in
the patriarchal family as a cultural-political creation.

> It is not the fact that woman are the primary reproduc-
> tive agents of society, in itself, that has led to their
> oppression, but rather that reproduction has taken
> place within a patriarchal power structure, has been
> considered a private rather than a social concern, and
> has been perceived as dictating women's entire lives,
> and as defining their very nature.[55]

Although Moller Okin did not analyze the political implications of the New Testament household code trajectory, she has documented that the Aristotelian political
ethics of natural inequality has shaped Western political
philosophy and society. A truly democratic society would
necessarily presuppose not only a radical change of the
patriarchal family but also a radical transformation of the
patriarchal churches into communities of equality and
mutual interdependence, since not only the family but also

the Christian churches have an important socializing function in American society.

The early Christian ethos of coequal discipleship in community could provide a model for the "new family" as an adult community of equality, mutuality, and responsibility for the home *and* for the "world." It could provide a model for the restructuring of the "patriarchal household of God" into a kinship community without clerical fathers and spiritual masters, a community not patterned after the patriarchal family. A feminist critical hermeneutics of liberation seeks to reactivate this early Christian ethos for today so that it can become a transforming historical model for the ordering of interpersonal communities, society, and the churches.

Because early Christian writers introduced the prescriptive Aristotelian ethics of patriarchal submission and patristic writers advocated an ascetic rejection of marriage and women, they together prevented a Christian understanding of marriage and family committed to the radical discipleship of coequals.[56] Insofar as the patriarchal household and misogynist asceticism, not the radical discipleship of women and men as equals, have become the structural models for the dominant institutional churches, Christian theology and communal praxis have not developed ecclesial structures capable of challenging the societal separation of the private sphere as the sphere of interpersonal love sustained by the self-sacrifice of women and the public sphere as a sphere of brutal self-interest and competition. Theology and church therefore failed to develop communal structures capable of socializing children into the Christian values of coequality in community, commitment, and discipleship, rather than into the cultural values and patriarchal roles of superordination and subordination, of masculinity and femininity.

Now that historical-critical scholarship has proven the New Testament household code texts to be a form of Aristotelian ethics, and feminist critical analyses have shown its destructive impact on women and the community of coequal discipleship, the church as the community of moral discourse is clearly challenged anew to incarnate the early Christian vision and praxis of coequality in community. True, the ethos of both coequal discipleship and the patriarchal pattern of submission can claim scriptural authority and canonicity. Both are expressions of believing communities in the first century and today. Insofar as the patriarchal pattern of submission has decisively formed Christian tradition and communal structures, it can claim even greater historical influence and institutional power for its own vision of how to live as a Christian community.

Nevertheless, feminist theology as a critical theology of liberation must reject the theological, scriptural claims of this patriarchal pattern because of its oppressive effects on the life of women and other subordinated peoples. A feminist critical hermeneutics has as its canon the liberation of *all* women from oppressive structures, patriarchal institutions, and internalized values. It therefore interprets, retrieves, and evaluates biblical texts and communal structures. It accepts or rejects them as well as their political-social functions according to its own canon of liberation. A feminist critical ethics that is committed to the liberation struggle of women and the whole church, therefore, insists that the ethos and praxis of coequal discipleship must transform the patriarchal household code ethics and its institutional structures if women and the Christian church are to have a feminist Christian future.

5.

Remembering the Past in Creating the Future
Historical-Critical Scholarship and Feminist-Critical Interpretation

RECENTLY I WAS INVOLVED in a discussion with students at one of the leading theological schools in this country. The women expressed their need for feminist biblical education and hermeneutics. One of them expressed their complaints well: "I have just come from this course that purports to introduce us to New Testament interpretation. But the guy talked a whole hour about historical-critical studies developed by German men in the last century. I am a second-career student and I do not have the time and the patience to bother with questions formulated by men in the past. What I want to do is to confront my own questions with the biblical text in order to find out whether it has something to say to my questions and to see what a feminist interpretation would do to my preaching and teaching of the Bible."

I was impressed and at the same time uneasy. I was impressed with this woman's articulate statement of her own theological goals challenging the established scholarship of the school. Remembering my own docility and "unconsciousness" as a woman student twenty years ago, I realized with pride that the work of the past decade in developing feminist theology and biblical interpretation had had some success in enabling women to articulate our own questions and to challenge the prevailing androcentric frameworks of scholarship. At the same time I was uneasy because the student was so certain that historical-critical scholarship had nothing to say to her own feminist theological quest and therefore could easily be discarded. I at least had experienced historical-critical scholarship as liberating, setting me free from outdated doctrinal frameworks and literalist prejudices. Had nobody bothered to make connections between her feminist theological questions and those of historical-critical scholarship? Or had I experienced historical-critical scholarship as opening up intellectual doors because I was prefeminist when I was introduced to it? Was she right in her assumption and had I just been co-opted into thinking otherwise? Or was I merely naive? I had always found the historical-critical method helpful for feminist critical interpretation and therefore assumed that resistance to such an interpretation was not because of the method but because of academic bias against women and our questions. What was it, then, that prohibited women in biblical studies from raising feminist questions as legitimate intellectual-historical problems? Were historical-critical methods such as textual criticism, philology, archeology, history of religions, tradition history, or form and redaction criticism at the root of the resistance to the feminist permeation of the field, or were the assumptions and frameworks of the historical-critical biblical discipline the source of the problem? And how much could method and conceptual frameworks be separated?

I. The Rankean Understanding of History

The quandary evoked by my conversation with women students was deepened upon my return home, where I found a German collection of essays entitled *Woman in Early Christianity.*[1] The contributions were written by my fellow students, with whom I had enjoyed exegetical discussions during the Schnackenburg doctoral seminar and theological-critical dialogues over *Frankenwein* during my student days. The volume pretends to be a response to the emancipatory tendencies of women in the church, but in reality it is an attack on a feminist critical hermeneutics that pursues, not the topical study of woman in the New Testament, but a feminist reconceptualization of early Christian history that could locate women's historical role not only at the margin of social-ecclesial relations but also at the center of them. Therefore prominent scholarship— the objectivity, reliability, and strictly historical approach of the authors—is stressed. "In order to engage in a discussion appropriate to the subject matter *(sachgerecht)*, an exact knowledge of the New Testament foundation is necessary. How was it in the beginning?" Established and "well-known" authors (none of them a feminist exegete!) explore the statements of the New Testament on *woman* with *wissenschaftlicher* objectivity and scientific methods. What early Christianity has to say about the role of woman is here *zuverlässig* (reliable), presented for the discussion on the "woman question" *(Frauenthema)* in the church. An additional contribution on feminist theology was especially solicited from a woman who, however, is not a biblical scholar and thus not an equal partner in the dialogue. Nevertheless, the editors insist that the objective of the volume is not a "direct discussion of present-day topics or hypotheses of feminist theology but rather the collection and interpretation of all New Testament texts on 'die Frau.' No mention is made that several scholarly collections and interpretations of these texts are already available and that the *wissenschaftlich* hermeneutic-methodological discussion has advanced beyond such a "topical" treatment of woman in the singular.[2]

Since I am not interested here in evaluating this particular collection of essays but in examining its male scholarly rhetoric against a feminist critical biblical interpretation, it is necessary to look at the understanding of historical-critical method and its goals presented there. This particular volume can serve as a case study to pinpoint the source of tension between historical-critical and feminist-historical biblical studies. The antiquarian understanding of historical-critical studies as it was formulated in the last century by Ranke comes to the fore in the introduction to the article on the household code of Colossians. This statement is quoted at length because it indicates the emotions and interests that inspire the rhetoric of a scientific, and well-established historical-critical scholarship that claims not to be influenced by present-day concerns.

Women who currently rebel ever more violently for their rights in society usually bring into play the so-called household codes *(Haustafeln)* of the New Testament when they present their generally harsh and resigned grievances against the traditions and institutions of a Christianity that in their opinion has considerably promoted and sanctioned the oppression of women. . . . Without question, therefore, in a book on the woman in early Christianity the *Haustafeln* must become an important topic. It is useful, however, at the very beginning to mark the terms to which the New Testament scholar must be bound if he *(sic)* does not want to gamble away his methodological credibility.

He *(sic)* may find his professional honor only in the fact that he does *not* interweave these ancient texts with the texture of modern emancipatory impulses and certainties, but rather seeks to explain them in correlation to their origin at the end of the first century A.D. This means especially that he can recognize their ethical quality only in a comparison with more or less vague, average injunctions for social behavior in later Hellenist antiquity. He must therefore be especially cautious not to explain away too quickly as conditioned by time or anachronistic all that which disturbs him today. His most important task will rather be to make felt exactly the offensive *strangeness* of these ancient expressions before the enlightened horizon of his own time.[3]

Such a rhetorical statement not only veils its apologetic aggression by claiming for itself historical objectivity but also advocates a nineteenth-century concept of history based on the assumption that the historian can "step out of his own time" and study history "on its own terms," "unencumbered by questions and experiences of "his own day." I deliberately use here the pronoun *he* for the historian, since women who have entered the field in the past hundred years or so could not do so on their own terms but only by adopting an androcentric conceptual framework and perspective that acknowledged women's experiences and intellectual questions only peripherally or not at all.[4] Therefore, women scholars no less than their colleagues subscribed to the Rankean definition of history as what actually happened. To bring their own issues to their intellectual work would have meant destroying the agreed-upon basis of this work. The feminist study of the Bible, therefore, did not originate with historical or biblical scholars in the academy but with women articulating their own biblical questions in their confrontation with anti-feminist biblical arguments used against them in their struggle for liberation.[5]

The true exegete is expected to examine all the material in a truly dispassionate manner in order to study the past "for is own sake" and to find out what actually happened. This ethos of historical-critical studies is also expressed in the following statement by the British scholar I. H. Marshall, which appeared in a book on New Testament methods of interpretation.

> By "historical criticism" is meant the study of any narrative which purports to convey historical information in order to actually determine what actually happened. . . . The phrase "what actually happened" is by no means free from difficulties of interpretation, but a common-sense view of it will suffice us in the present discussion.[6]

The task of the historical exegete is therefore to interrogate the texts "in order to construct a picture of the event which they reflect, a picture which will be in itself historically coherent and which will also serve to explain the wording of the sources."[7] If it is assumed that the New Testament texts mirror the reality of early Christian women and give us an accurate picture of their involvement in early Christianity, then it is the "scientific" exegete who establishes objectively *wie es am Anfang war*. Moreover, since the work of Dilthey, the historian is expected to enter "sympathetically" into the minds or consciousness of historical persons to empathize with their motivations, intentions, and actions, to see them from their own point of view and not from that of the inquiring historian. Historical "objectivity" compels interpreters' to put themselves into the place of historical agents whose "historicity" means that their values, actions, and motivations are alien to the contemporary inquirer.[8]

It seems no rapprochement is possible between a feminist historical-critical and a positivist-historical understanding. Insofar as an understanding of biblical historiography prides itself on being impartial and value-neutral, objective and descriptive, scientific and antiquarian, it must reject any feminist reconstruction of early Christian history as "ideological" and "influenced" by present-day concerns. A feminist-critical interpretation in turn cannot acknowledge as valid the claims and assumptions made by such biblical scholars if it does not want to relinquish its own interest in the past and its own heritage. Although value-neutral, descriptive historical-critical scholarship can "collect" the passages on "Woman," it cannot conceive of women as equally involved in early Christianity as men were. It cannot do so because it understands its androcentric sources as "data" and its own androcentric language and narrative as totally divorced from contemporary concerns. It overlooks thereby what Bultmann insisted on, that no understanding is possible without preunderstanding. Scholarship claiming to be "objective" and "realistic" is not more value-free and less ideological because it hides its "subjectivity," "cultureboundedness," and "contemporary interests" from itself. Such a Rankean[9] definition of historical-critical biblical scholarship overlooks the hermeneutical-critical insights of the past one hundred years and neglects recent methodological discussions in New Testament scholarship.[10] It also disregards the epistemological debate among philosophers of history on the possibility and the specific character of historical knowledge.

II. The Narrative Character of Historical Knowledge

The debate between the "objectivist-realist" and the "constructionist" direction in historical scholarship highlights two different perceptions of what we can know historically.[11] The objectivist direction holds the Rankean view that the past can be known scientifically and objectively.

Historical facticity and theological truth can become identical. Historians assemble historical facts, drawn from historical sources and evidence. They use this collected evidence to discover and relate what actually happened at a certain time and certain place. Historians succeed at least sometimes in describing with "scientific objectivity" the actual events of the past.

The constructionist epistemology of historical knowledge stresses its "time-boundedness" and "linguisticality," which make it impossible for us to know the "real past" as we would know an object in the present. Neither the description of "data" nor the establishment of "historical facts" is scientifically verifiable because the description of historical data and facts is "narrative-laden." Statements of historical fact do not emerge by themselves as ready-made mirrors of past events. In order to make statements of historical fact, scholars must draw inferences based in part upon their "data" or "sources" and in part upon their general understanding of human behavior and the nature of the world. They not only deal selectively with their historical sources in order to present a "coherent" narrative account, but also ascribe historical "significance" to their "data" in accordance with the theoretical model or perspective that "orders" their information.[12] This emphasis corresponds with the insight of the hermeneutical discussion that the interpreter is not able to step outside the "hermeneutical circle."

In *History and Social Theory* Gordon Leff repeatedly states the criteria for a "good history." According to him historical "objectivity" consists, not of "pure" facts or "data," but of the dynamic interrelation between the information gleaned from the sources and the "unifying vision" of the interpreter. Historians gather all available evidence, account for its correct use, and order it within a framework of reasoning. Nevertheless, historians argue from evidence as opposed to events accessible to our experience. In the attempt "to make the past intelligible," the historian must go beyond the events in an act of "intellectual recreation."[13] In doing so the historian shows at once why, for example, "Caesar's crossing of the Rubicon was significant for posterity and what it meant for Caesar and his contemporaries." In order to do so the historian must have a theoretical frame of reference and must construct a model that is at once a comparative and an ideal construct.

> . . . the letters on a stone or a piece of parchment or the remains of a medieval village or a treatise by a schoolman, do not of themselves provide more than the data on which the historian sets to work; and in order to make them into historical facts, i.e. what he [sic] assumes to have been the case—he [sic] has to employ a full critical and interpretative apparatus of selection, evaluation, interpolation and rejection—which rests upon inference as opposed to observation, and hence can never pass beyond a high degree of probability."[14]

The relationship between thought in the present and statements about the past is constituted by the explanatory models or ideal-typical constructs that help us to organize our knowledge of the past and give meaning to it. These explanatory models can be either *structural* models, which are static in nature and focus on the dominant elements of a given social formation, such as feudalism, fascism, or the Renaissance, or they can be *developmental* models, which provide a structural-temporal line for narrative presentation. Models can be chosen consciously or they can remain unconscious; they can be used in isolation or in combination with one another.

Reconstructive inferences, selection of "data," and ascription of historical significance depend on both the choice of explanatory models and the rhetorical aims of the work. Hayden White has pointed out that historians "shape" their material not just in accordance with a narrative framework of preconceived ideas but also in response to the narrative discourse in general, which is *rhetorical* in nature.[15] In the very language historians use to describe their projects they provide a certain amount of explanation or interpretation of what this information *means* and also give a more or less overt message about the attitude the reader should hold toward the historical "data" and their interpretation. White agrees with Claude Lévi-Strauss that history is never just "history of" but always also "history for." It is "history for" in the sense of being told with some ideological goal in mind and in the sense of being written *for* a certain group of people. "The clue to the meaning of a given historical discourse is contained as much in the *rhetoric* of the description of the field as in the *logic* of whatever argument is offered."[16] Therefore the traditional distinction between "historical facts" (data) on the one hand and their interpretation (or the story told about the facts) on the other hand is misleading. It obscures the epistemological difficulty of distinguishing between these two levels.

Historical discourse itself is the actual "combination of facts and meaning which gives to it the aspect of a *specific* structure of meaning that permits us to identify it as a product of one kind of historical consciousness rather than another."[17] Thus two levels of historical discourse can be distinguished: The "surface" level of the discourse consists of the historical facts *and* their interpretation and the "generic story type" comprises the conceptual model to which the events are to be likened but which is not always consciously chosen. This "generic story type" can be detected in the rhetorical "clues" and "emotion-laden" words pointing to the figurative element of the discourse.

Since every account of the past is mediated by the style of language in which historians describe the historical field, a nonrelativistic account of historical reality is not possible. Rankean "realism" also was "relativistic" insofar as it required that historians view the past on "its own terms" or "for its own sake." Objectivity meant thinking one's way back into the consciousness of the historical epoch and getting "outside" one's own time and culture, viewing the world of antiquity, for example, "from its own perspective," as ancient people would have understood it. Therefore the historical-critical exegete had first to find out, for example, what the text of the New Testament *meant* in its historical context , whereas the preacher's task was to "apply" it and to explicate what it *means* today.[18] But this division overlooks that we know "more" about the Greco-Roman world than the early Christian might have known. It also neglects the hermeneutical insight that "stepping outside" one's own time and culture is not only impossible but also not desirable. History is not written today for people of past times but for people of our own times. The antiquarian understanding of history is not only epistemologically impossible but also historically undesirable. What needs to be rediscovered is the understanding of history not as artifact but as "historical consciousness" for the present and the future, a historical consciousness that understands historical knowledge in terms of the *topos* coined by Cicero: *Historia magistra vitae (De Oratore libri tres* II.36).[19]

Historical knowledge is not only "history for" but also knowledge dependent on the self-image of the social group for which historians speak and to which they belong. Far from recording what actually happened with the utmost objectivity and value-neutrality, historians have written history for the dominant groups in society. History was conceived as a history of empires and wars, or as the history of political or cultural heroes, and it was written in order to instill national pride or cultural hegemony. History was made and written by the "winners"; the oppressed and vanquished of the past do not have a "written" history.

Social historians have pointed out that we know little about the everyday lives of most groups of ordinary people. Our sources rarely speak about the experiences and contributions of slaves, serfs, prostitutes, working-class people, or colonialized peoples. American historians have shown that historiography in this country was from its inception occupied with questions of public policy and sought to imbue Americans with a sense of national pride. "From the days of the first doctoral program at Johns Hopkins, where 'History is past politics' was a slogan inscribed on the seminar room wall, historians have defined their subject as a record of the public and political aspects of the American past."[20] Feminist historians in turn have pointed out that most histories were written as if women did not exist or as if we were some rare and exceptional creatures on the fringes of American social life.

Intellectual historians, moreover, have shown that the three eminent historians of "realist historiography," Ranke, Meinecke, and Croce, were antiprogressive and politically reactionary. Ranke developed his notion of history in opposition to the revolution of 1830 and for the sake of the Prussian governmental and social elites. Although he stated "his historical urge to survey the whole (of modern history) from a detached viewpoint," he maintained that the separation and independent development of the European states, which were fortified by the centrifugal force "of the national principle," express "'the secret of world history' and thus serve as the conservative general counterpart to the 'general movement of democracy' which would dominate or homogenize the individual states."[21] In Meinecke as well as Croce, realist historicism is also intertwined with clearly conservative positions: "In Meinecke it is tied to a nineteenth-century conception of the national state of romantic inspiration on the one hand and Bismarckian politics on the other hand; in Croce it is intertwined with a form of liberalism which is not only ademocratic but clearly antidemocratic."[22] Thus historical discourse is not only "narrative-laden" but intrinsically linked to the specific sociopolitical reality in which it arises and to the sociopolitical location of the historian who produces it.

The past is not a continuum of given facts we can rediscover by mere objective observation, but rather discloses itself only to us if we put specific questions to it. Historians are never able to free ourselves totally from our own experiential presuppositions or institutional interests, and we should not even attempt to do so. What makes our work interesting and fruitful are the specific questions, concerns, insights, perspectives, and commitments that compel us to study a certain epoch of the past or to choose from the complexity of historical reality those elements that enable us to make the causal link between the past and our world. Therefore, all historical discourse and judgment stands

as it were with one foot rooted in the self-image of a certain group in society. The current values, interests, and traditions of the group to which the historian belongs and which make up his [sic] audience determine not only the subject matter the historian

examines and perspective he [sic] brings to bear on
it but also the explanatory models he [sic] uses to
conceptualize and explain the multifarious historical
phenomena before him [sic]. This is precisely what
provides historical judgments with the meaning and
relevance they have for a reader who is confronted by
them as a human being whose interests are primarily
determined by the intellectual context of the present.[23]

Not value-neutrality but public consciousness and
discussion of one's values, interests, commitments, presuppositions, and sociopolitical location are required for
historical discourse.[24] The self-conscious relativity and
multiformity of historical inquiry create conditions for
maximum communication across ideological lines. Nevertheless historical narrative and judgments are not totally
relativistic and can be distinguished from mere fictive
accounts. They are open to and necessarily subject to
scholarly scrutiny. They can be tested in terms of the source
material they draw on and in terms of the assumptions and
models underlying them. In other words, historical judgments are intersubjectively understandable and intersubjectively verifiable. Three criteria for publicly testing
historical knowledge are proposed. First, to what extent
have relevant sources been utilized and how much has the
present state of research been considered? Second, how
much has the account reached an optimal plausible integration of all available historical information? Third, how
logically rigorous, consistent, and coherent is the use of
explanatory heuristic models, and are they reasonably free
from self-contradictions? Explanatory models must be
"adequate" to the historical object under consideration.[25]
Public discussion of historical constructions as "history
for" can be a valuable aid in clarifying the self-understanding of social groups as active participants in history. Liberation theology has therefore insisted that historical-critical
biblical scholarship begin with an analysis of its own
historical-political situation and with the articulation of
one's "hermeneutical preference" rather than with the
pretension of "objective," "truly historical" scholarship.
This demand is in accordance with historical thinking.

> The social value that history as a discipline provides lies in subjecting prevalent historical assumptions to rational analysis, thereby testing for validity the understanding that social groups have of themselves. Historical thought is valuable not only as an anti-dogmatic weapon . . . but also as a critical and rational instrument of inquiring into the historical dimensions of contemporary value systems and of self-understanding of contemporary societies.[26]

Public historical discourse not only among historians but also among biblical interpreters and theologians would reduce the danger that communications will be broken off either with one's own tradition or with the traditions of different cultures, religions, and times. Finally, public historical discourse can make it possible to step "somewhat" outside our present horizons, by allowing us to remain conscious of our human and historical relativity and potential. Studying the past to recover its unfulfilled historical possibilities becomes a primary task for historical inquiry.[27] It enables us to keep our future "open" in light of our historical heritage and identity.

In conclusion, I have attempted to show that a certain reified understanding of history is contrary to feminist interests, for it excludes women's questions and thus women as historical subjects. The truly historical understanding of historical inquiry on the contrary invites active feminist participation in the writing of human history in order to keep "open" our unfulfilled historical possibilities for a more human future. Moreover, this understanding of historical inquiry is not just open to feminist participation but also, more appropriately, to biblical interpretation. It enables us to see the Bible not just as a history of Israel or the ministry of Jesus and the early church but also as history for certain communities and people. It allows us to integrate biblical history and biblical theology as historical rhetoric for believing communities.[28] It allows for a feminist-critical interpretation of the Bible as a historical rhetoric for women-church.

Rapprochement between feminist biblical and academic biblical scholarship is possible only when biblical-historical scholarship has taken cognizance of the new developments in historical epistemology and critical hermeneutics and is *willing* to shed its outdated assumptions of "scientific factuality" and its pretensions of "positivist objectivity," as well as honestly to articulate its own social-ecclesial-political locations and interests.[29] In short, such rapprochement is possible only when established biblical scholarship recognizes its male-centeredness as a scholarly, intellectual "handicap" and in a process of public consciousness-raising has the chance to develop a truly "historical consciousness."

III. Historical-Critical Feminist Interpretation

Although women have participated in the production and teaching of historical-critical scholarship for more than a hundred years, only now do we seek consciously to do such scholarship and biblical interpretation not just for the academy or the church but for all women affected by biblical religion, and especially for women-church.[30] In order to do so, I would argue, we need to use the methods and means of historical inquiry developed by historical-critical scholarship while at the same time scrutinizing and contesting its androcentric philosophical-theological presuppositions, perspectives, and goals.

Feminist studies as an intellectual discipline has only begun to articulate the challenge that such a shift in scholarly commitment and purpose implies for historical knowledge and for a truly human historical consciousness. Feminist scholars in all areas of intellectual inquiry are in the process of inaugurating a scientific revolution that engenders a paradigm shift from an androcentric—male-centered—world view and intellectual framework of discourse to a feminist comprehension of the world, human culture, and history.[31] While androcentric scholarship takes *man* as the paradigmatic subject of scientific knowledge and defines women as the "other," or as the object of male scholarship, feminist scholarship insists on the reconceptualization of our language as well as of our intellectual frameworks so that women as well as men become the subjects of intellectual inquiry.

The shift from an androcentric to a feminist construction of the world and of history challenges the established intellectual frameworks of androcentric scholarship and questions their claim to objectivity and value-neutrality.

But insisting that women be entered into sociology [or history] as its subjects, we find that we cannot escape how its practices transform us into objects. As women we become objects to ourselves as subjects. . . . So long as "men", "he", and "his" appeared as the general and impersonal terms locating the subject of sociological assertions, the problem remained invisible. We had learned to "enter" our subjectivities into sentences beginning "he" and to disattend our sex under the convention—applying only to women since it is irrelevant for men—that the pronoun was in this context neutral. Once we had understood, however, that the male pronoun did indeed locate a male subject for whom women were constituted in the sociological relation outside the frame which organized his position, the appearance of impersonality went. The knower turns out after all not to be "abstract knower" perching on an Archimedean point but a member of a definite social category occupying definite positions in the society.[32]

Feminist studies therefore maintains that established scholarship as androcentric scholarship is not only *partial*, to the extent that it articulates male experience as human experience, but also *biased*, to the extent that its intellectual discourse and scholarly frameworks are determined only by male perspectives primarily of the dominant classes. This feminist claim runs counter to the assertion of traditional historical-critical biblical scholarship that prides itself on being impartial, objective, and value-neutral. Recognizing its sociopolitical location and public commitment, a feminist biblical interpretation must therefore utilize historical-critical methods for the sake of presenting an alternative interpretation of biblical texts and history for public scholarly discussion and historical assessment. In order to do so, we must develop a hermeneutics of suspicion to be applied both to the contemporary scholarly historical discourse and to that of the biblical writers. The feminist hermeneutics of suspicion understands androcentric texts as selective articulations of men often expressing as well as maintaining patriarchal historical conditions.

As androcentric texts, our early Christian sources are theological interpretations, argumentations, projections, and selections rooted in a patriarchal culture. Therefore they need to be read critically for their theoretical-theological androcentric tendencies and their polemical theological patriarchal functions. Such texts must be evaluated *historically* in terms of their own time and culture and assessed *theologically* in terms of a feminist scale of values. A careful analysis of their androcentric tendencies and patriarchal functions, nevertheless, can provide clues for constructing a historical model of interpretation that does justice to the egalitarian and patriarchal tendencies and developments in the early church. The critical analysis of androcentric biblical texts needs to be utilized positively for a feminist reconstruction of Christian origins in order to arrive at a feminist biblical consciousness. A hermeneutics of suspicion must lead to a feminist hermeneutics of remembrance.

In the past decade women historians have articulated the theoretical problem of *how* to move from androcentric text to historical context and of *how* to write women into history. Scholars of American history in particular have pointed out that the task of feminist historical interpretation is to place the lives of all women at the center of historical reconstructions and at the center of efforts to transform and change societal structures and institutions.

> Feminist historians are asking what it was like to be a woman at various times in history and are exploring women's subjective responses to their environment. . . . In short, new approaches to women's history are at-

tempting to integrate women into the mainstream of American historical development rather than isolating woman as a separate category.[33]

Feminist historians, therefore, point out that the literature on women in history is too often limited by narrowly focusing on *woman* as a topical or heuristic category rather than exploring new conceptual frameworks that would allow us to place women at the center of human social relations and political institutions. Furthermore, feminist historians question the androcentric scholarly evaluation of "historical significance" and point out that many of the historical sources on women are not descriptive but prescriptive. Women are neglected in the writing of history although the effects of their lives and actions are a reality in history. Ideas of men *about* women, therefore, do not reflect women's historical reality, since ideological polemics about women's place, role, or nature increase whenever women's actual emancipation and active participation in history become stronger.

Some feminist historians, therefore, propose a theoretical framework that can maintain the dialectical tension of women's historical existence, namely, to be at one and the same time active participants in history and objects of patriarchal oppression. Since gender dimorphism is generated by such patriarchal oppression, it is not "natural" but social.[34] Therefore we must reject heuristic concepts such as "biological caste" or "women's experience" as essentially different from that of men because these categories render women passive objects because of biological differences or of male dominance.

We must seek instead heuristic models that explore women's historical participation in social-public development and their efforts to comprehend and transform social structures. It is not "biological" sex differences but patriarchal household and marriage relationships that generate the sociopolitical inferiority and oppression of women. Patriarchy is at home in the patriarchal household and its property relationships rather than in innate biological differences between women and men.[35] Wherever the "private sphere" of the patriarchal house is sharply delineated from that of the public order of the state, women are more dependent and exploited; in societies in which the boundaries between the household and the public domain are not as sharply drawn, women's positions and roles are more equal to those of men. While the public sphere is stratified by class differences, the domestic patriarchal sphere is determined by sexual role differences and dependencies.

Although some scholars of women's history and religion have postulated matriarchy as an oppositional societal structure to patriarchy, others have constructed heuristic models to measure women's power and influence within patriarchal history. In order to do so, they seek not only to restore women to history and history to women but also to reconceptualize history and culture as the product and experience of both women and men. Women's experience of solidarity and unity as a social group is not based on our biological differences from men but on our common historical experiences as an oppressed group struggling to become full historical subjects. This theoretical framework allows women to locate our strength, historical agency, pain, and struggle within our common historical experiences as women in a patriarchal society and family. It also allows the scholar to account for variations in social status, class, and cultural identity.

This feminist theoretical framework encompasses a "view of women's historic role as located simultaneously in the center of social relations and at the edge of them." It thereby allows us to explore patriarchy as the source of women's oppression as well as of women's power. The interest of women in their own social history is similar to a colonialized people's interest in unearthing their own past.

The search to understand collective conditions and the relations of race to the dominant society has enabled blacks to locate their strengths, their social importance, and the sources of their oppression. Furthermore, this process has provided an analytical framework for recognizing their unity through historical experience, rather than simply through their racial difference from the ruling caste.[36]

Like historians of other oppressed groups and peoples, feminist historians seek to comb androcentric records for feminist meaning, reappropriating the patriarchal past for those who have not only suffered its pain of oppression but also participated in its social transformation and development. As biblical historians, we can do so because the canonization process of early Christian writings has preserved both the patriarchalizing texts of the New Testament and the early Christian traditions or texts that permit a glimpse of the egalitarian-inclusive practice and theology of early Christians. These texts are like the tip of an iceberg, indicating a rich heritage now lost to us. Therefore we must cease interpreting the women's passages in the New Testament in isolation from their historical-ecclesial-social contexts. What is necessary is a systemic interpretation and historical reconstruction that can make the submerged bulk of the iceberg "visible."[37]

The scant references to women as well as the inconsistencies in our New Testament sources still indicate that women were members and leaders in the early Christian movement and that the formation of early Christian traditions and their redactional processes followed certain androcentric interests and theological perspectives. This androcentric selection and transmission of early Christian traditions seems to have engendered the historical marginality of women. New Testament texts are not an accurate reflection of the historical reality of women's leadership and participation in the early Christian movement.

It is important to note that the redaction of the Gospels and of Acts was undertaken when the patriarchalization process of the early church had begun. Since for various reasons the authors were not interested in extolling women's and slaves' active participation in the Christian movement, we can methodologically assume that the early Christian writers transmit only a fraction of the possibly rich traditions of women's contributions to the early Christian movement.[38] Much of the information and many of the traditions about the agency of women in the beginnings of Christianity are irretrievable because the patriarchal transmission and redaction process considered these stories and information either as insignificant or as a threat to the gradual "patriarchalization" of the Christian movement. A feminist reading of biblical texts and the reconstruction of their historical-social worlds therefore need to utilize all available historical-critical methods and means of inquiry, in order to reconstruct the historical-theological tendencies and rhetorical aims of the redactional process of the history of the tradition.

If the "silences" about women's historical experience and theological contributions in the early Christian movement are produced by androcentric language, texts, and historical models of reconstruction, then we must find ways to "break" the silences of the texts and to derive meaning from androcentric historiography and narrative. Rather than understand the texts as an adequate reflection of the reality about which they speak, we must search for rhetorical clues and allusions that indicate the reality about which the texts are silent. Rather than take androcentric biblical texts as informative "data" and objective reports, we should understand them as social constructions by men and for men and read their "silences" as indications of the historical reality of women about which they do not speak directly. Rather than reject the "argument from silence" as valid historical arguments, we must carefully read the clues of the text pointing to a different historical reality and integrate them into a feminist model of historical reconstruction in such a way that we can give voice to their silences and understand them as part of the submerged traditions of the egalitarian early Christian movement.[39]

Like other sources, androcentric biblical texts are part of an overall puzzle that must be "fitted" together in creative critical-historical interpretation. It is crucial, therefore, that we challenge the androcentric model of early Christian history by assuming instead a feminist pattern for the historical mosaic, one that allows us to place women as well as men at the center of early Christian history. This feminist critical method could be likened to historical-theological "detective" work in that it does not rely on the obvious "facts" or "invent" its evidence, but is engaged in an imaginative reconstruction of historical reality. Or to use the metaphors of the feminist poet Adrienne Rich: In order to "wrench meaning" from androcentric texts and history we have to "mine" "the earth-deposits of our history" to find the "bottle amber perfect," "the tonic for living on this earth the winters of this climate."[40] A feminist hermeneutical method and process for unearthing biblical feminist history, for "entering an old text from a new critical direction," is not just a "chapter in cultural history" but an "act of survival." In deconstructing dominant male language and traditions,

> feminist interpretation restores the complexity of historical and symbolic processes. Feminist interpretation draws its strength from recognizing the common tradition as common, the product of many labors and subjectivities. But this recognition in turn compels feminist interpretation to take the tradition seriously and to struggle to appropriate it. The point of feminist interpretation is not to reject the tradition in toto, but rather to reappropriate it in the name of those whose participation has been governed by injustice, those who have been excluded not so much from its workings as from its dominant subjective voice.[41]

In conclusion, in order to break the hold of androcentric biblical texts over us, it is necessary to uncover the mechanisms and incoherencies of such texts, to see the inconsistencies of our sources, to elaborate the androcentric projections and political-theological functions of such texts and their contemporary androcentric interpretation. In order to recover the historical defeats and victories, sufferings and contributions, of our biblical foremothers and foresisters as our own heritage and historical power, we must insist on new feminist models for historical reconstruction.

Such models of historical remembrance must replace the androcentric models of biblical history and help us to re-vision Christian origins and biblical theology in a feminist perpsective. Biblical history and theology can no longer be undertaken only for men but must also be written explicitly for women. We must not seek an increase in antiquarian information but an increase in historical consciousness and biblical remembrance.

Rather than integrating itself into the Rankean paradigm of historical biblical scholarship, a feminist historical reconstruction of early Christian origins seeks to recover the literary or rhetorical historical paradigm as well as the understanding of history as remembrance and memory for those who were participants in it. The significance of the latter distinction comes clearly to the fore in discussions on the historical significance of the Holocaust. Responding to revisionist historians who argue that this event has never taken place,[42] the Jewish historian Pierre Vidal-Naquet has addressed the relationship between history and memory most forcefully. He argues that

> today we are witnessing the transformation of memory into history. . . . My generation, people about fifty, is probably the last one for whom Hitler's crimes are still a memory. That both disappearance and, worse still, depreciation of this memory must be combated seems to me obvious. . . . But what are we going to do with this memory, that while it is our memory, is not that of everybody?

But rather than pursue the political implications of this statement, he insists on a clear-cut distinction between memory and history. He relates that during the war his father had him read Chateaubriand's famous article in the *Mercure* of July 4, 1807, from which he quotes:

> In the silence of abjection, when the only sounds to be heard are the chains of the slave and the voice of the informer; when everything trembles before the tyrant . . . this is when the historian appears charged with avenging the people.

But Vidal-Naquet disagrees with Chateaubriand on the task of the historian. He insists:

> I still believe in the need to remember, and in my way I try to be a man of memory; but I no longer believe that historians are charged with "avenging the people."

> We must accept the fact that the war is over, that the tragedy has become, in a way, secularized.[43]

Although I would not insist that revenge is the historians task, I would maintain that history and remembrance should not be separated as if "the war is over." Neither anti-Semitism nor misogyny are movements and events of the past. To recover biblical history as memory, and remembrance as history for women, does not mean abandoning critical historiography but deepening a critical understanding of historical inquiry, conceiving of historiography as a memory and tradition *for* people of today and tomorrow. We participate in the same struggle as our biblical foresisters against the oppression of patriarchy and for survival and freedom from it. We share the same liberating visions and commitments as our biblical foremothers. We are not called to "empathize" or to "identify" with *their* struggles and hopes but to continue *our* struggle in solidarity with them.[44] Their memory and remembrance—rediscovered and kept alive in historical reconstruction and actualized in ritual celebration—encourage us in historical solidarity with them to commit ourselves to the continuing struggle against patriarchy in society and church.

6.

Toward a Critical-Theological
Self-Understanding of Biblical Scholarship

THERE IS A STORY about a priest and his economical housekeeper who used to combine all the leftovers of the week for a Sunday night dinner. Once the priest forgot to say grace and she reprimanded him: "A priest shouldn't forget to say grace before dinner." "Oh, that's not necessary," the priest retorted. "The food has been blessed six times already."[1] Addressing a topic as broad as the self-understanding of biblical scholarship and its critical transformation may seem like offering a warmed-up dinner. Most readers of this book are probably familiar with the sentiment that contemporary historical-critical scholarship has its roots in the Enlightenment, that its pathos is antidoctrinal, rationalistic-objectivistic, and academic-Germanic. Conservative Biblicists therefore reject it as godless humanism, which tampers with the very words of God "Himself."

While some liberation theologians reject historical-critical scholarship as the enterprise of middle-class white academics, some feminist theologians denounce it as inherently male and thus useless for women. In the preceding chapters I have maintained to the contrary that a critical-feminist liberation theology must challenge biblical scholarship to become more critical as well as more theological in its own self-understandings and praxis.[2] If feminism is a movement for liberation and change, then we must seek to transform male scholarship and to use it in the interests of those who are oppressed and whose oppression is legitimated by citing Sacred Scripture as the inerrant Word of God.

I. The Present Crisis in Biblical Scholarship

A feminist critical hermeneutics of liberation challenges historical-critical scholarship to become more critical of biblical texts as well as of its own function. It therefore must pay attention not only to the ways in which patriarchal theological mind-sets and structures are encoded in the biblical writings and canonized as the direct Word of God, but also to the ways in which its own presuppositions, commitments, and interests perpetuate patriarchal oppression and dehumanization. Feminist hermeneutics challenges biblical scholarship to become more critical of its own professed objectivism and value-free stance.

In doing so a feminist theology of liberation also challenges biblical scholarship to become more theological in the precise sense of the word. If Christians understand the Bible as divine revelation, then biblical interpretation is a theological task in the strictest sense. Insofar as the Bible as Holy Scripture speaks about God, biblical scholarship must develop a critical method and hermeneutics that does not "render God" as a God of patriarchal oppression.

Some of my colleagues might interject that it is not the task of biblical scholarship to raise these questions. The biblical scholar is an exegete and historian, not a theologian or preacher. He—and many still say *he*—must work out what the text meant to the author and original readers and find out what happened and how it happened in biblical history, but then leave it to the preacher or the teaching authority of the church to say what the text *means* for us today. Disciplined historical-critical scholarship thus restricts itself to the task of philological, historical, and literary analysis. The biblical scholar addresses the issues and questions raised by the community of historical-literary critical scholars, while the theologian and preacher address the questions of the contemporary community of faith.[3] This argument for the division of labor between historical-critical biblical scholarship and theology overlooks that biblical scholarship, insofar as it calls itself biblical, expresses not only a historical-literary claim but also a theological self-understanding. New Testament studies do not define themselves as explorations of Christian literature, history, and religion of the first century but as studies of the New Testament, and thus they are not only canonical studies but also relate to the contemporary Christian community that reads the New Testament as Holy Scripture.[4]

The questions explored by historical-literary biblical scholarship and those raised by believers and churches today are often so disparate that it is sometimes impossible to "apply" a historical-critical interpretation addressing questions of scholarship to a pastoral situation. The proliferation of commentaries to the lectionary testifies to this predicament of biblical scholarship and biblical preaching. No wonder that readers of the Bible continue to adhere to a literalist reading promising "instant" pietism and that ministers skip historical-critical exegesis for the sake of actualizing rhetorics.

Others might argue that historical biblical scholarship cannot engage in a discussion of its scholarly methodological self-understandings because the very basis of biblical scholarship as *historical*-theological scholarship is being challenged today. To engage in a self-critical discussion would mean jeopardizing the critical gains biblical scholarship has made in the past two hundred years or so. At biblical conferences and in publications a war seems currently being waged, a war similar to that fought among literary critics for several decades after the advent of the New Criticism.[5]

For instance, Augustine Stock argues for a replacement of the historical-critical method through the synchronic approach of the New Criticism or structuralism.[6] Whereas the diachronic method of historical-critical exegesis seeks to reconstruct the historical context of the biblical text, to find the original text, to reconstruct what actually happened by means of textual and historical criticism, and to narrow down the diverse meanings of the text to the one "meaning intended by the author," linguistic structuralism elaborates the "meanings perceived by the readers" and the New Criticism insists that the text receives its meaning not from outside itself but that "the text means what it says and it says what it means." Therefore, Stock argues, we must work with the text as we have it rather than postulate antecedent sources, traditions, or external social-historical "influences."

Leland White's theological appraisal of historical-critical exegesis is positive, stressing that it has generated historical consciousness and pluralistic understandings in contemporary theology and church.[7] In contrast Charles Davis declares categorically, "Historical criticism of the Bible, while it may still have a glorious future as a branch of history, would seem to be near the end of its career in theology."[8] Moreover, "since theology is concerned with the meanings of biblical texts themselves and not with their use as clues in an investigation alien to their original intention, it is now time for theology to bow historical criticism out and bow literary criticism in."[9] However, the discussions on the New Criticism and the "New New Criticism" among American literary critics and among biblical scholars have progressed beyond the either/or stance proposed by Charles Davis.

Another group of scholars holds that historical-critical scholarship should render a useful service to church and theology by restricting itself to the scientific discussion of what "the text meant" and to the historical reconstruction of what actually happened in the life of Jesus or the early churches, because the present-day danger is not too much historical critique but rather literalist pietism and rightist dogmatism. Since literalist Biblicism and traditionalist fundamentalism are not restricted to Roman Catholicism, it might be helpful to look at Raymond Brown's analysis for its relevance to all churches.

According to Brown, Roman Catholic scholarship has moved through three distinct periods in this century. The first period was plagued by the official Catholic rejection of biblical criticism (1900–1940). The second period began in the 1940s and climaxed with the acceptance of biblical studies in Vatican II and with the changes in the church after Vatican II. This period is characterized by a gradual acceptance of historical-biblical scholarship by Roman Catholicism, although the wide-ranging implications of this scholarship are still not clearly perceived. The present period of biblical criticism, beginning in the 1970s, will have to deal with these ramifications for Catholic ecclesial self-understandings, doctrine, theology, and practice. Brown fears that biblical criticism could be suffocated by pietism and exaggerated traditionalism, which occurred at three other crucial moments in church history—the time of Jerome, the School of St. Victor in Paris, and Richard Simon—when biblical criticism began to have an impact on Roman Catholic theology.[10]

In order to safeguard the influence of biblical criticism in the church, Brown suggests a division of labor between the biblical scholar and the teaching authority of the church. Biblical scholarship has the task of saying what a text *meant* in its own time and thereby of enabling Catholics to understand, for example, why other Christian churches have a different church order or doctrinal position. The teaching office of the church, decides not what the text *meant* but what it *means* today. Therefore, the meaning of a passage in the literal-historical sense, as worked out by exegesis, might be something quite different from what the official church interpretation of that passage for today teaches. For instance, he argues that the understanding of what Matthew or Luke *meant* in telling us about the origins of Jesus in the infancy narratives can be the same among Catholic and Protestant scholars approaching the texts with the same methods, whereas the present-day *meaning* of these texts is quite different for a Catholic and Protestant Christian because the Catholic tradition and doctrine of the "Virginal Conception of Jesus" inform the understanding of a Catholic today.[11] What the text *meant* for its authors and what it has come to *mean* in a church, therefore, can stand in creative tension.

The argument in favor of historical-critical exegesis has come full circle here. While historical criticism developed in confrontation with the dogmatic understandings and doctrinal authority of the institutional church, Brown stresses that it has to remain relatively independent and restricted to biblical scholars in order to avoid a conflict with the teaching authority of the church. Only time can tell whether the argument will protect Roman Catholicism from a spiritualistic pietism and exaggerated traditionalism emerging within the official church that is intolerant of historical distance and pluralism.

In order to understand this emphasis on a clear distinction between "what the Bible meant and what it means" as a crucial issue in historical-critical biblical scholarship, we must uncover the roots of this present self-understanding, especially in American biblical scholarship. James Barr[12] has pointed out that American biblical scholarship has restricted the task of the exegete to working out what the text *meant* in response to the so-called biblical theology movement that flourished after World War II until the early sixties.[13] Common to the entire program was a strong reaction against the ways in which the Bible had been studied under the aegis of "liberal" theology. Analytical, philological, and often dry historical exegesis, with its great reliance on grammar, style, and source criticism, its rationalism and evolutionism as well as its tendency to understand biblical materials in terms of the cultural environment and surrounding religions, had lacked for many an explicitly theological and existential concern.[14]

In contrast with this approach in historical-critical scholarship and dogmatic-systematic strictures, the biblical theology movement asserted the uniqueness of biblical thought and theology, by emphasizing three points.[15] First, the movement stressed its opposition to philosophy and philosophical modes of thinking, and opposed the systematizing tendencies of dogmatic theology. Biblical thought was a living organism and could not be reduced to a dogmatic system. The movement was parallel to the neo-orthodox movement in other areas of theology. At the same time it argued that biblical thought as Hebrew thought, was distinctly different from Greek thought that dominated dogmatic thinking. Systematic theology, in turn had been distorted by its adoption of Greek categories.

Second, the movement stressed the unity of the Bible and maintained that the New Testament had to be solely understood in terms of Old Testament–Hebrew thought. Unfortunately, this emphasis entailed a negative perception of early Judaism, the dominant environment in which the New Testament originated, because intertestamental Judaism was also influenced by Greek thought. Related to this emphasis on the unity of the Bible was an emphasis on the distinctiveness of the Bible compared to its environment. The cultural-religious parallels were viewed as only partial and isolated phenomena.

Finally, the theological basis for this emphasis on the unity and distinctiveness of the Bible was the understanding of God's revelation in history. The whole of history was conceived as *Heilsgeschichte*—salvation history. Revelation in history was assumed to be typical for Hebrew thought: a notion unknown to the extrabiblical world but characteristic of the entire Bible.

Although the biblical theology movement appears not to have developed its own particular methods, two emphases have been characteristic of its general method of exegesis: On the one hand it stressed word study and on the other it engendered a division of labor within theology because it could not integrate theological claims and historical method.

Word-study method was based on the assumption that it was possible to trace the outlines of biblical Hebrew thought through the words of the Hebrew language. Greek words, when they came to be used in Christian writings, were assumed to take on Hebraic content and to mirror the Jewish-Christian-Hebrew thought pattern.[16] To link the New Testament more closely with Hebrew thought, scholars assumed that biblical writings were either translations from a Hebrew or Aramaic source or that their forms and outlines were based on forms and books of the Hebrew Bible. One of the major tools for biblical theology was Kittel's *Dictionary of the New Testament*, which traced words of the New Testament to their Hebrew roots.[17] Although this method has been thoroughly debunked by modern semantics and structuralism, it is still widely in use, probably because it easily allows an extraction of "theological thought" from biblical texts without requiring the student to enter into the literary-historical complexities raised by historical-critical exegesis. Moreover, although modern linguistics has rejected the evolutionism of the word-study method its emphasis on the "text" and and its anthropological essential substructures to the detriment of its historical context allows a similar easy access to the biblical texts and their religious constructs without the problems related to historical-sociological reconstructions.

In contrast to the history of religions approach, the biblical theology movement insisted that the Bible should be interpreted for believing communities today, and not simply be explained with a dry philological or historical statement about the past. Yet at the same time this movement maintained that biblical theology must not simply work with modern categories and reconstructive models but must submit itself to those of the Bible and Hebrew thought. In contrast to liberal theology, the movement maintained that only a theocentric method concentrating on the kerygma is appropriate for biblical interpretation. In Old Testament studies, for example, Eissfeldt urged a twofold method—historical investigation of Hebrew religion and systematic presentation of the timeless truth of Old Testament revelation in classical theological categories.[18] In New Testament studies Cullmann found the key to the theology of the New Testament in the concept of time, maintaining that the categories of time and history rather than of essence, eternal or existential truth, and normative principles are decisive for biblical theology.[19] As Otto Betz summed up, "The difficulty with Biblical theology lies in the fact that it comprises a diversity of witness interrelated with history rather than a theological system. Yet Biblical theology should take its principle of exposition from the Bible itself. It is not possible to grasp the Hebrew way of thought in the Bible with the systematic principle which came from Greek thought and wove itself into Christian dogma" and ethics.[20]

Writing in 1960 and 1968 on American New Testament scholarship in the past fifty years,[21] Henry J. Cadbury and R. M. Grant respectively defend and exalt historical-critical inquiry but mention biblical theology only in passing. Ironically, Cadbury characterizes the biblical theology movement as focusing on the Gospel *about* Jesus and on the unity of the Old and New Testaments, but he does not mention a single proponent by name. The quest for the historical Jesus has, according to him, been supplanted by a concern for interpretation on a different plane. "Not what Jesus did and said but what his figure meant or means is nowadays to the fore. History is still used of him—but it is the cosmic fact of history—of *Heilsgeschichte* that many are concerned with, not with the minor features of his life and teaching.[22] Even more sweeping is the comment of R. M. Grant.

> The basic method among my teachers, I believe, can be put very simply. It was to try to find out what writings meant to their authors and first readers and to find out, as far as history was concerned, what happened and how it happened. . . . It is true that during the quarter of a century since then there has been a tremendous emphasis upon the theological meaning of the NT and of early Christian literature in general. This emphasis now reminds me of the Augustan propaganda literature determined to exalt the empire at the expense of the republic.[23]

After describing American scholarship as characterized by "common sense" combined with a daring "to damn the torpedoes" and "full steam ahead," he suggests that the American motto might be "Investigate, then invest," since Americans like to keep their feet not only on the ground but also "in the ground," as their preference for archeology and paleography rather than philosophical theology indicates. He concludes his article by stating that the work and permanent achievement of the period were made by those whose "goal was understanding rather than proclamation. They did not sell their birthright as critics and historians for what has been called 'a pot of message.' "[24]

Ernest Cadman Colwell is more constructive in his assessment of New Testament theological scholarship, since as a member of the Chicago school he is more open to form criticism. Yet he bemoans that biblical theology is too strongly influenced by philosophy and systematic theology. He therefore suggests that it should be called systematic-biblical theology in order to distinguish it from a future historical-biblical theology, which he saw emerging from the post-Bultmannian discussions of the "new quest for the historical Jesus." While systematic-biblical theology, in his opinion, has only unsatisfactorily dealt with the problems arising from the historical nature of Christian faith, historical-biblical theology will be—as he hopes— "more sophisticated in theology and philosophy than some of our past studies, and it will be historically more comprehensively rigorous than much of our contemporary study."[25]

In his influential article on biblical theology that appeared in 1962 in *The Interpreter's Dictionary of the Bible*, Krister Stendahl sought to do justice to the historical-critical as well as contemporary theological concerns of biblical scholarship. He proposed two distinct tasks and three stages for doing biblical theology. The first task was descriptive.[26] The exegete must give an objective historical analysis and description of the "data" of the Bible. Stendahl stresses objective analysis and scientific description of "what the text meant" in its historical context as the primary task of the exegete. The task of the theologian is the hermeneutical task which was to attempt a "translation" or application of biblical statements and thoughts into the modern situation and thought horizon. These two tasks, the exegetical working out of "what the Bible meant" and the hermeneutic-theological stating of "what the Bible means" today, must be strictly kept apart in order to do justice to the historical-critical task of the exegete and the theological-interpretive task of the contemporary biblical theologian. This distinction was widely accepted and, as we have seen, still operates in biblical scholarship.

Stendahl also proposes a three-stage method for biblical theology.[27] "With the original in hand, and after due clarification of the hermeneutic principles involved, we may proceed toward tentative answers to the question of the meaning here and now. . . . How much of the two last stages should belong to the discipline of Biblical studies or to what extent they call for teamwork with the disciplines of theology and philosophy is a practical question which in itself indicates the nature of the problem. If the three stages are carelessly intermingled, the theology as well as the preaching in our churches becomes a mixed or even an inarticulate language."[28]

Before Stendahl moves to the discussion of the hermeneutical question, he elaborates as the key for the unity of the Old and New Testaments, as well as a common basis for today, the "sacred history" of the people of God.[29] Descriptive biblical theology thus gives him the hermeneutical key that allows for a common bond between the contemporary church and that of the period of the New Testament. Consequently, he maintains that the pulpit is the place or "life situation" where "the meaning of the original meets with the meaning for today."[30]

Yet we must not overlook that Stendahl stresses the distinction between "what the text meant" and "what it means" in order to emphasize that "the descriptive task has no claim or intention toward the normative. This is of utmost importance, since anything called 'biblical' has a tendency to participate in the authority assigned to the Bible in Christian churches."[31] In other words, Stendahl maintains that the biblical exegete and historian does not seek to answer the normative question of what a writer's theological statements "mean" in a timeless and absolute manner. Insofar as Stendahl defines the problem of what the text means in a normative manner and ascribes to it an ahistorical or transhistorical character, which must be elaborated by the systematic theologian and preacher, his proposal anticipates that of Raymond E. Brown, who ascribes the normative task to the teaching office of the church. Stendahl's theological *interest* points of course in the opposite direction from that of Brown's. As H. Boers has stressed, the Reformation maintained that the Bible was not part of the contemporary life of the church but belonged to the historical past, in order "to establish the Bible as the sole base and norm over against the contemporary church by means of which to judge and renew it." Yet in doing so the theologians of the Reformation "set a process in motion which made it increasingly questionable how a collection of documents from the past could be normative for the present."[32]

In his response to Stendahl, A. Dulles recognizes this and therefore stresses continuity.

What the text meant to the inspired author and as taken up in the inspired tradition is still normative. While the church's understanding of Scripture is far from static, it is not so fluid that the meaning in biblical times has lost all binding force. If the original meaning is in any sense normative, the basis of Stendahl's dichotomy is seriously impaired.[33]

At the same time he concedes that a claim to the normative value of "what the Bible meant" would mean a "confessional" approach in biblical theology. He also maintains an objective, scientific, noncommitted approach on the level of factual biblical history and the description of the religious history of the Bible. He is able to do so because he adopts R. de Vaux's distinctions of three levels of biblical work: the levels of historical, history of religions, and theological inquiry.[34] Yet contemporary discussions on biblical method and hermeneutics question such dichotomies in the self-understanding of biblical scholarship as historical-textual interpretation.

II. The Role of the Historical-Critical Method

Biblical scholarship agrees widely on what kinds of methods and procedures are involved in working out an "objective" description of what the text meant within its sociohistorical context.[35] Critical biblical scholarship demands that we give adequate reasons for the assertions we make, that we be cognizant of the research pertaining to the interpretation of a certain biblical text, and that the various disciplines involved in the historical-critical method control our analysis, scholarly argument, and historical reconstruction. The "external" disciplines of the historical-critical method are philology, archaeology, and ancient history, which correlate the biblical text with evidence from independent sources.[36] Textual, source, form, tradition, and redaction criticism deal with the "internal" analysis of the text.

Linguistic, rhetorical, architectonic, literary, genre, structualist, or deconstructionalist analyses have been added in recent years to enable the interpreter to understand the text as text and to chart the literary dynamics of a biblical book more fully.[37] Thus, the historical-critical method has become a historical-literary critical method that defines the enterprise of contemporary biblical studies. While at the beginning literary critics absolutized the synchronic reading of the biblical text over the diachronic readings of traditional historical-critical studies, scholars are reaching a greater balance in their methods. Since many historical texts, especially biblical texts, have predominantly social communicative and not primarily aesthetic functions, their social-historical setting also needs to be explored in order to understand their meanings.[38]

While the New Criticism and certain directions in structuralism deny any scientific-theoretical possibility for a diachronic reading of texts, epistemological discussions among literary critics and historians have shown that an abstractionist-positivist understanding of language and texts is not justified.[39] Any literary theory must place the literary work at "the meeting point of two 'axes' of literature: the rhetorical axis of communication connecting author and reader and the mimetic axis of representation connecting language and information.[40] By extending the horizontal rhetorical axis beyond the implied author and reader, the actual author and readers can be seen against their "world" as a source of motivation or a field for action. By extending the vertical mimetic axis, language systems can be understood as different ways of utilizing the world as reservoir of signs, while "world views" emerge as the result of employing signs to represent them. In other words, the critical study of biblical texts begins with language and literary analysis but cannot eschew social-historical analysis if it intends methodically to elaborate and scientifically to describe "what the text meant" in its social-ecclesial-historical situation.

A "scientific" reading of the Bible makes the text the object of its attention. It places "distance" between the text and the interpreter, the world of the text and that of the exegete, the world view of the text and that of the contemporary believer. This "distancing" effect is part of a "historical consciousness" that allows the community of faith "to disengage itself" from its past as well as from its present sociocultural embeddedness and biases.

Leander E. Keck has therefore argued that historical analysis and reconstruction is a "major factor in the community's capacity to come to terms with its own past—precisely in relation to its canon."[41] It is historical-critical analysis that allows the Christian church, for example, to recognize its Jewish roots and therefore to reject anti-Semitism in its teachings and practice as well as in the past and present biblical interpretations of exegetical commentators. In short, the methods of historical-critical scholarship and its diachronic reconstructions "distance" us in such a way from the biblical communities, writers, and texts, that they critically and theologically relativize not only them but also us. Thus, historical criticism enables contemporary Christian communities and scholars to become self-critical.

Biblical texts have a long history of reception, interpretation, and use. In the process they have been understood in terms of certain dogmatic assumptions, cultural ideologies, or church practices. Contemporary believers approach them with their own doctrinal questions and spiritual interest. Certain biblical texts are quoted over and over again so they have lost their meaning and have become stereotypical injunctions. By "distancing" the text historical-critical interpretation seeks to make it "alien" to our own experiences, expectations, interests. This is an important *theological* function of historical-critical scholarship insofar as Christian faith and community is bound to the historical person Jesus of Nazareth and to the witness of his first followers and believers.[42]

Thus historical-critical interpretation of the Bible can function as a theological corrective in the process of the reception of biblical texts by contemporary Christian communities.

1. It asserts the meaning of the original witness over later dogmatic and social usurpations, for different purposes.

2. It makes the assimilation of the text to our own experience of parochial pietism and church interests more difficult.
3. It keeps alive the "irritation" of the original text by challenging our own assumptions, world views, and practice.
4. It limits the number of interpretations that can be given to a text. The "spiritual" meanings of a biblical text are limited by its literal historical meanings.

Whereas biblical exegesis and historical reconstructions are concerned with "what the text meant," biblical hermeneutics seeks to explore the dialectic between past and present, biblical texts and our own contemporary understandings influencing the process of interpretation.[43] It seeks to illuminate *how* "translation" of "what the text meant" to "what the text means" today takes place in the act of interpretation and proclamation. While Stendahl proposed that exegesis and normative interpretation are the two poles of the hermeneutical dialogue, Ricoeur distinguishes explanation and understanding as the two poles of the hermeneutical arc. Explanation is truly methodical, but understanding is the first step toward bringing back to life a particular text.[44] As we have seen, in historical-critical description interpreters must seek to silence their own subjectivity and strive for detached objectivity that excludes the existential-religious questions the Bible addresses. This historical inquiry is necessary because of its distancing function, so that the text can speak for itself and not merely mirror the ideas of the interpreter. Yet this form of exegesis is either only preliminary to the interpretive act or restricted to the historical-critical exegete in contrast to the systematic theologian or the ecclesiastical teaching office.

Hermeneutical theory rejects this dichotomy in the process of understanding and questions the subject-object relationship between the interpreter and the text. It conceives of the interpretive task as a continuous dialogue between the interpreter and the text or the "world" of the text that has as its goal a fusion of horizons. While so-called descriptive exegesis seeks to eliminate the subjectivity of the interpreter in order to produce an objective description of "what the text meant," the hermeneutical circle situates interpreter and biblical text within an ongoing and corrective dialogue.[45] To understand what the "text means" is to understand "what the text meant" and vice versa. Therefore, no division of labor between the descriptive biblical exegete and the interpreting systematic theologian is possible.

R. Bultmann has already argued that understanding is only possible because we share certain existential concerns and anthropological presuppositions with the authors of biblical texts.[46] The interpreter's mind is not a *tabula rasa*, but before we attempt to understand how an author deals with a certain subject matter or before we become interested in a text, we must have a certain common experience, understanding, or relation to the issues and "world" expressed in the text. Just as we must have an appreciation of music in order to understand a textbook on musicology, so must the biblical interpreter have a certain relationship to the intention and subject matter of biblical texts. Therefore "presuppositionless" exegesis is not only not possible but also not desirable.

As Gadamer has pointed out, every interpreter stands within a historical tradition of interpretation that provides her or him with certain preunderstandings and prejudgments.[47] It is necessary to bring these pressuppositions and prejudgments to consciousness so that the temporal and cultural distance between the interpreter and the text comes to the fore.[48] Only the awareness of the differences between their respective horizons allows the distinctive message of the text to reshape the questions, concepts, values, and horizon of the interpreter. In the process of interpretation "the rights of the text" must be guarded, the acceptance or consent of the text sought if a "fusion" or "communion" of horizons is to be achieved. To enter the hermeneutical circle with a prejudice forecloses dialogue with the text and makes an encounter with it impossible.

In short, understanding takes place in a circular manner: Interpretation and answer to a certain extent determined by our presuppositions and prejudgments as well as by the questions we ask and how we ask them. Our questions and readings in turn are confirmed, extended, or corrected by the text. A new question then grows out of this understanding, so that the hermeneutical circle continues to develop in a never-ending spiral. Illegitimate prejudice refuses to alter its preconceived questions and judgments when new insights and understandings are derived from the text. The refusal to be challenged by the text reduces the hermeneutical spiraling process of interpretation to a repetitive circle. Nevertheless, P. Stuhlmacher insists:

> Historical-critical exegesis is not in and of itself theological interpretation of scripture. But it can be such when it is hermeneutically reasoned out as an interpretation of consent to the biblical texts, and when it is carried on theologically in regard for the enduring hermeneutical relevance for the Third Article of the Apostles' Creed.[49]

Since the *New Hermeneutic* has links with the thought of Bultmann, it is concerned with the relevance and effectiveness of Christian preaching. Yet, it is more concerned with the "linguisticality" and the "rights of the text" *as text* so that the text can become both an illumination of and a challenge to present experience. "The preacher 'translates' the text by placing it at the point of encounter with the hearer from which it speaks anew into his [*sic*] own world in his [*sic*] own language."[50]

Hermeneutical theory does not stress critical consciousness as much as it emphasizes surrender and fidelity to the biblical text. This becomes clear, for example, in Sandra Schneiders' proposal that seeks to utilize Gadamer's hermeneutical theory for Roman Catholic biblical interpretation. She argues that exegesis is not a science but an art. Just as there are techniques for playing a musical instrument, so there are techniques for analyzing a text. But these techniques must be integrated into and must serve the artistic process of interpretation.

Just as the score remains normative for the musician, and the rendition is always judged by the score and by the history of interpretation of the piece, so the interpretation of the exegete remains always under the judgment of the text and of the faith tradition of the church.[51]

Schneiders argues that philosophical hermeneutical theory also enables us to relate the biblical interpretation of the "ordinary" Christian to that of the exegete. She likens the interpretation of the believing community to the enjoyment of listening to a symphony and that of the exegete to the musicians who reenact the musical score of the symphony. "Unless *someone* can play Chopin the ordinary person will never have the chance to appreciate his music."[52] In a similar fashion it is the exegete who makes the meaning of the text available to the community. Finally, she identifies biblical interpretation with the "excess of religious meaning because the biblical text is a mediation of meaning about the relation of God and the human race."[53]

This delineation of the relationship between exegete and preacher on the one hand and the "ordinary" believer on the other expects both too much and too little from biblical scholarship. It ascribes too much to biblical scholars and preachers by comparing their work to that of artists performing a symphony. Insofar as "ordinary" members of the community can read, they are able to understand and interpret a text.[54] Insofar as they are able to read the text itself, not only the "score" of a work is accessible to them, but also the "making of music" because the technique of reading is the equivalent to the technique of playing the violin. "Ordinary" believers may not be accomplished as "artists," but exegetes and preachers are also not "artists" in interpretation just because they have the techniques and knowledge of historical-critical interpretation. To the extent that "ordinary" Christians do not have sufficient philological, historical, archeological, theological, or literary skills of interpretation, their "readings" will necessarily be limited or distorted. Nevertheless, their "reading" might often be more accurate than those of the exegete because they and not he or she share the religious experience or the social *Sitz im Leben* of a text.

In short, I would maintain that the "ordinary" believer and the professional biblical interpreter or preacher should not be related to each other as nonexpert and expert, or as consumer and producer of meaning. Rather than artists making the meaning of biblical texts accessible today, biblical scholars are more like cultural critics who subject both the historical-critical interpretations of their colleagues and of "ordinary" believers and preachers to a critical evaluation and hermeneutics of liberation.[55]

The consensual-hermeneutical self-understanding of biblical scholarship seems, therefore, too restrictive, insofar as it eliminates the critical task of biblical interpretation or relegates it to historical-critical method defined as description or explanation, and at the same time excludes it from the "artistic reenactment" of biblical texts and meanings. This critical aspect of biblical scholarship must be maintained, because we are never able to say what the text means without saying what it meant and vice versa. Rather than eliminating preliminary assumptions and presuppositions, we must make them conscious in a public critical discussion and interpretation.

Biblical students, therefore, should not only be trained in historical critical analysis, they must also learn to reflect methodologically on their own presuppositions, interests, prejudices, and commitments as well as on those of biblical scholars or theologians. Students must learn to analyze critically the implicit frameworks and interests of scholarly, pietistic, and ecclesiastical interpretations of the Bible. Historical criticism becomes theological criticism whenever this task is taken seriously, as Paul Hanson has pointed out.

Throughout the world, in bodies large and small, similar retrenchment and declaration of immunity to criticism are occurring. More emphatically in the present moment than in any time in the recent past, professors of the Bible and biblically-trained pastors and church leaders are called back to one of their responsibilities that has slipped into neglect. They must subject to ongoing criticism the ways in which Scripture is being used and the sources of the presuppositions guiding both the scholarly and the popular use of the Bible, whether they are derived from dogma, cultural fads, national ideolgies, or philosophical assumptions. In holding biblical theologians to account, we can measure their activities against the two qualities required of all professions, moral responsibility and self-criticism of guiding principles and presuppositions.[56]

At the same time such critical-theological interpretation of Scripture must not only evaluate the contemporary interpretations of biblical texts but also move from "a hermeneutics of consent" to a "hermeneutics of suspicion" in order not only to understand biblical texts and their worlds of meaning but also to evaluate them in terms of a critical theology of liberation. Already A. Schlatter has called for such a critical biblical theology.

We can never give past occurrence absolute power to shape us so that the telling of what was could render our judgment superfluous, or tradition replace our own reflection. . . .We are always called to an act of reflection, in which our own personality forms its judgment.[57]

The perception of biblical scholarship as the critical-theological evaluation of present and past interpretations and articulations of the religious experiences of biblical people is being developed increasingly by liberation theology, especially in the context of a critical feminist theology of liberation.[58]

III. The Challenge of Liberation Theology

In contrast to hermeneutical theology, liberation theologies maintain that the goal of biblical interpretation is not only understanding but also ultimately a new, different praxis.[59] Biblical interpretation must not aim solely at the understanding of biblical texts and their meanings. It must not seek merely for a "hermeneutics of consent" but for a new liberation praxis in the community of believers. Thus "the meaning of a text is disclosed not only in reflection upon it but also in concrete social action based on it."[60] Moreover a critical-theological evaluation, not only of contemporary biblical interpretations and their interests but also of biblical traditions and writers, derives its critteria of evaluation from the theoretical and practical commitment to the contemporary struggle for liberation.

Thus liberation theologies challenge biblical scholars, preachers, and the entire Christian community to articulate their theological commitment and engagement in the liberation struggle of those who suffer from patriarchal oppressions: from racial, sexual, colonial, economic, and technological exploitation. The basic methodological starting point of liberation theologies is the insight that all theology knowingly or not is by definition always engaged for or against the oppressed.[61] Intellectual neutrality is not possible in a historical world of exploitation and oppression. If this is the case, then theology cannot talk about human existence in general, or about biblical theology in particular, without identifying whose existence and whose God is meant. This "advocacy stance" of all liberation theologies is the major point of disagreement between liberation and academic theology.[62]

Academic biblical scholarship with a positivist posture rejects liberation-theological interpretations of the Bible as "ideological" and "unscientific" because they are influenced by present-day concerns. A feminist or liberationist interpretation in turn cannot acknowledge the claims and assumptions made by positivistic scholarship if it does not want to relinquish its own interests in women's biblical past and heritage. While a value-neutral, detached, scientific biblical scholarship, for example, can collect the biblical passages on *woman*, it cannot conceive of women as equally involved in shaping early Christian origins and articulating its religious vision. It cannot do so because it accepts androcentric biblical sources as "data" and "evidence" and its own androcentric linguistic interpretive models and narrative as totally divorced from contemporary concerns.[63] Scholarship claiming to be "objective" and "neutral" is not more value-free and less ideological because it hides its subjectivity and contemporary interests from itself.[64]

In contrast with interpreters who claim to be free of institutional interests, liberation theologians maintain that theology as well as biblical interpretation are never done in an institutional and personal vacuum but consciously or not are always "interpretation for." In order to sustain the "advocacy stance" the scholar of the Bible must first understand her own experience, adopt a clear political-social-theological analysis and then act upon her commitment to the oppressed and the marginalized.

Segundo has outlined four decisive steps in the liberation-theological hermeneutic of the Bible. First, our experience of reality leads us to ideological suspicion, which then applies itself to the whole ideological superstructure in general and to theology in particular. Next, this new way of experiencing theological reality leads us to the "exegetical" suspicion that the prevailing interpretations of Scripture have not done justice to all biblical texts and to the reality about which they speak or are silent. Finally, we interpret Scripture according to our new theological perspective, which sheds fresh light on all previous readings of the text.[65] Let us consider a specific instance. Women who have undergone a process of consciousness-raising and have become self-identified as women will experience first a tension between their own self-understanding and the position of women in society and church, which then leads us to scrutinize prevailing androcentric theological systems. Next, this new insight that theology was formulated by men in the interest of patriarchal male structures will lead us to question the prevailing androcentric interpretations of Scripture. Finally, the reading of Scripture from a feminist theological perspective will result in a new interpretation of Scripture that takes into account both the androcentric language and patriarchal tendencies of the biblical writers.

Liberaticn theologians maintain further that their pre-understanding—the option for the poor—is not *eisegesis* but exegesis, since this message is already found in the text: The God of the Bible is the God of the poor and oppressed.[66] At this point it becomes apparent that the critical hermeneutical task of feminist theology is more complicated, since it cannot state without qualification that the "God of the Bible is the God of women,"[67] because there is considerable evidence that the Bible not only was used against women's liberation but also had no clear "option" for women's liberation.[68] Segundo is aware that some biblical texts are oppressive formulations but he argues that they must be understood as responses of faith in certain historical situations. Therefore, he maintains that biblical interpretations must reconstruct the "second-level learning process" of biblical faith. Faith is identical with the total process of learning ideologies; it is an educational process throughout biblical and Christian history. This second-level, educational process expresses the continuity and permanence of biblical revelation, whereas ideologies document the first-level, historical character of biblical revelation. "In the case of . . . the Bible we learn to learn by entrusting our life and its meaning to the historical process that is reflected in the expressions embodied in that particular tradition."[69]

It is obvious that Segundo's interpretive model stands within the hermenutical-dialogical paradigm. He shares with neo-orthodoxy the hermeneutical presupposition that scriptural traditions are meaningful, that the process engendered by the Bible can be trusted and can therefore claim our "empathy" and "consent." Yet in contrast to neo-orthodox theology, Segundo does not claim that the content of biblical texts is *eo ipso* meaningful and liberating; he maintains that only the educational faith process engendered by them is meaningful and liberating.

But by separating content and process to such a degree, the "advocacy stance" for the oppressed cannot develop its full critical potential. Feminist theology therefore insists that we have to bring to bear a critical evaluation and "hermeneutics of suspicion" both upon the content and the process of biblical interpretation as well as upon the biblical texts themselves. The critical evaluation of literary works demanded by feminist literary critics must also be carried out by a critical-theological feminist interpretation of biblical texts and their historical impact and effect.

The traditional formalist assumption has been that the reader should 'give in' to the vision imposed by the work. . . . I believe that rather than suspending disbelief and allowing the ethics of the text to be imposed upon one by the form, one should enter into the fictional world ... only if it seems that the characters and situations depicted therein are authentic and just. Whenever one cannot accept the ethics of the text, one cannot accept the aesthetics.[70]

Let me restate this theologically. Whenever one cannot accept the religious, political, and personal ethos and ethics of a biblical text, one cannot accept its authority as revealed and as Holy Scripture, that is, if one does not want to turn the biblical God into a God of oppression. Such a critical evaluation of biblical texts cannot locate inspiration in the text, not even in its "surplus" or polyvalence of meaning. Instead it must place it in biblical people and their contexts. As J. Barr has proposed, inspiration must be understood "as the inspiration of the people from whom the books came."[71] Inspiration cannot be located in texts or books, but its process is found in the believing community and in its history as the people of God. The feminist liberation theologian would qualify this statement by insisting that the process of inspiration must be seen as the inspiration of those people, especially of poor women, struggling for human dignity and liberation from oppressive powers, because they believe in the biblical God of creation and salvation despite all experiences to the contrary.

Therefore, feminist biblical hermeneutics stands in conflict with the dialogical-hermeneutical model developed by Bultmann, Gadamer, and the New Hermeneutic, because it cannot respect the "rights" of the androcentric *text* and seek for a "fusion" with the patriarchal-biblical horizon. Its goal is not "identification with" or "consent to" the androcentric text or process of biblical reception but faithful remembrance of and critical solidarity with women in biblical history. In other words, it does not focus on *text* as revelatory word but on the story of women as the people of God. Its "canonical" hermeneutics insists that the people of God are not restricted to Israel and the Christian church but include all of humanity, because the Bible begins with creation and ends with the vision of a new creation.[72] This challenge of feminist theology to hermeneutical theology is well expressed in John Cobb's review of David Tracy's position:

> Hermeneutical theology makes sense as long as we believe that our classics are essentially adequate to our needs. But what if they are not? What if our need is for really new thinking and practice? Our classics point ahead to such newness, and in that very important sense they are adequate. But the new thinking we need about Jews and women breaks the boundaries of what is appropriately called hermeneutics.[73]

The feminist and liberation theological challenge to the hermeneutical paradigm in biblical and theological interpretation does not mean that "historical criticism has come to the end of its theological career" as Charles Davis argued. The opposite seems to be the case. Rather than making historical-criticism obsolete, the new challenge forces theologians to relinquish their understanding of the Bible as a "classic" and to develop a critical hermeneutics rather than a "hermeneutics of consent." It also forces historical-critical biblical scholars to sharpen their critical acumen by utilizing the epistemological insights of historical and literary criticism.

Since I have addressed the question of a critical feminist hermeneutics of the Bible in previous chapters,[74] I will here point out that the feminist liberation-theological challenge too an objectivist-factual and hermeneutical-textual-consensual model of biblical scholarship provokes a more critical understanding of the historical and literary task of biblical interpretation. Three insights of theoretical discussions among historians and literary critics appear to me crucial: (1) the rhetorical character of historiography as "history for," (2) the definition of literary criticism as "criticism for," and (3) the understanding of history as "what happened" and "what shall be remembered."

The debate between an "objectivist" and a "constructionist" historical epistemology highlights two different perceptions of what we can know historically.[75] As noted above, the objectivist direction holds to the Rankean view that the past can be known scientifically as "it actually was." In this view, historical facility and theological meaning and truth are interchangeable. A constructionist epistemology stresses in turn the "time-boundedness" and "linguisticality" of historical knowledge. Statements of "historical facts" are not simply mirrors of past event. In order to make statements of "historical fact," scholars must work with information derived in part from their sources and with interpretive models influenced by their general understanding of human behavior, nature, and the world. Historians deal selectively with their material and ascribe historical significance to their sources in order to present a "coherent" historical narrative.[76]

Reconstructive inferences, selection of data, and ascription of historical significance depend also on the rhetorical aims of the work. Historians "shape" their materials in accordance with a narrative framework of preconceived ideas and response to the narrative discourse in general, which is rhetorical in nature. History is never simply "history of" but always "history for." History is told with an ideological goal in mind, and is written for a certain group of people.[77]

History and biblical interpretation is not written today for people of past times but for people of our own time. The antiquarian, objectivist view of biblical texts and history is epistemologically incorrect and historically undesirable. We need to recover the perception of history, not as artifact, but as historical consciousness for people of the present.

American historians have shown that historiography in this country has been occupied from its inception with questions of public policy and with imbuing Americans with a sense of national pride and unity.[78] Feminist historians in turn have pointed out that most historical accounts are written as if women did not exist or as if we were marginal to social life. The obvious reason is that history was written by educated white men. Indians and blacks received the same treatment as women. Similarly, Church history was written primarily as "clerical" history, because male clerics were not only writing but also reading these historical accounts.

In short, the insistence of liberation theology on an explicit "advocacy stance" brings into the open only what has always been at work in historical interpretation. A critical feminist liberation theology therefore does not obstruct but enhances the self-understandings of critical biblical scholarship when it insists that all theological and biblical scholarship begin with an analysis of its own historical-political situation and with an expression of its own "hermeneutical option" rather than with the deceptive posture of representing detached, neutral, scientific and unbiased scholarship.

Since the Bible is a document of biblical communities of both the past and the present, biblical scholarship must respond to both academic standards and those of biblical communities; it must be done *for* biblical communities today.[79] The intellectual freedom from doctrinal control is to be used as creative freedom *for* nurturing the faith and vision of contemporary biblical communities struggling for liberation. While the historical-factual self-understanding of biblical scholarship ascribed the central role in interpretation to the detached and scientifically trained historian, the paradigm of hermeneutics accorded the primary role in biblical interpretation to the preacher and pastor. Yet it appears that a new model of biblical interpretation is emerging in which the members of believing communities have a central role. This is the case in Christian base-communities of Latin America and in feminist biblical communities of women in North America. This new direction in biblical interpretation is oriented less to scientific validation and stature in the academy,[80] and less to authoritative proclamation in the church. As "interpretation for," it seeks to formulate a new liberating biblical vision that can sustain, encourage, and challenge biblical communities of faith. The authority of the Bible is not that of control but that of enabling power.

Salvation as the possibility of freedom and peace has not only to be acknowledged, it also has to be grasped and practiced by the reader. The text only helps to create possibilities; it is for the reader to realize them in life.[81]

If historical interpretation is not simply descriptive but always rhetorical, then we cannot simply strive for "identification" or "empathy" with the text in order to understand it. We must also seek to evaluate its meanings and significance. Since biblical texts claim authority of Holy Scripture, biblical exegetes must pay special attention to the rhetorical aims of the text and to those of its subsequent interpretations in the history of the Church. While form, redaction, and literary criticism analyze the theological dynamics and aims of a story, author, or text, biblical interpretation must also move to a critical evaluation of its own theological rhetoric.

Wayne Booth has recently argued that the literary critic must interpret and evaluate a classic work of art in terms of justice.[82] He thereby seeks to revive a responsible ethical and political criticism that recognizes the ideological limitations of a great work of art. Such a criticism does more than evaluate the ideas or propositions of a work; it seeks to determine whether the very language and composition of a work portray persons stereotypically and thus unjustly without itself criticizing such a literary portrayal. What does language of a text do to the reader who submits to its "world of vision"? Does it promote dehumanization and injustice, or does it enhance our freedom to become more fully human? Similarly biblical interpreters, especially those who teach and preach today, must critically evaluate terms of a Christian scale of values both the rhetorical aims of biblical texts and the rhetorical interests emerging in the history of interpretation or in contemporary exegesis. Historical-critical interpretation needs to be complemented by a controlled and disciplined theological-critical evaluation in order to become *biblical-*critical interpretation. Biblical scholarship has fought hard for, and therefore always prized, its freedom *from* dogmatic and ecclesiastical control or pietistic bias. Liberation theology now challenges biblical scholarship to articulate

its own self-understanding more fully not only as "freedom from" but also as "freedom for" critical evaluation.[83]
A "freedom for" would presuppose a public discussion
of the interests, theological commitments, and theological
assumptions of biblical scholars. It would mean, moreover,
that there is a need to develop a scale of values for judging
which theological texts may be preached or accepted
today as the Word of God and which should not. For example, I argued in chapter 3 that no biblical patriarchal
text that perpetuates violence against women, children, or
"slaves" should be accorded the status of divine revelation
if we do not want to turn the God of the Bible into a God
of violence.[84] That does not mean that we cannot preach,
for instance, on the household code texts of the New
Testament. It only means that we must preach them critically in order to unmask them as texts promoting patriarchal violence. Naturally this evaluation would presuppose
that biblical students learn to discuss the interpretations
of biblical scholars and become skilled in the analysis of
contemporary situations and ideologies.

Finally, liberation theology challenges biblical scholarship to complement its Rankean view of history as "what
actually happened" with a view of history as "what shall
be remembered." Paul Hernadi has pointed out that this
view of interpretation and historiography is based on an
understanding of history as "continual translation."[85]
All original sources and documents at the disposal of historians as well as the work in which they are engaged are
verbal accounts of nonverbal, historical events. To the
extent that historians "communicate," they translate the
idiom of events past into the idioms and perspectives of
present discourse. They continually translate the sealed
book of "how it really was" into interpretation after interpretation disclosing "how it shall be remembered." In
other words, historians and interpreters narrate past events
according to a present critical consciousness.

History as "what shall be remembered" seeks to make
us comprehend and choose between different types of
theological goals and purposes, in order to lead us to a
historical praxis. "While conservative science claims, 'All

things are determined' and radical myth insists, 'All things
are purposeful,'" the art of scientific historical interpretation suggests that "causality and teleology are comple-
mentary idioms."[86] While factual historical criticism seeks
to trace lines of causal determination in the past, theo-
logical-historical criticism views the past from the perspective of contemporary participants facing the future.[87]
Liberation movements have pointed out that it is a sign of
oppression not to have a written history and historical self-
identity. History is not a collection of facts or a meaningless chronicle, but either a means of domination or the
heritage of a people that looks to the past for its vision of
the future. Therefore, if oppressed peoples are to have a
future, freedom, and autonomy, they must recover their
historical roots and base their solidarity on a common historical self-understanding.[88]

The perception of history as the memory of a believing
community comes close to the remembrance of the Exo-
dus and the Lord's Supper enjoined to the Jewish and
Christian communities, respectively. Yet as James Sanders
has pointed out, the reactualization of the central remembrances of the biblical communities depends on one's "taking sides." In a "constitutive reading," for example, of
Luke 4:16–30, one automatically takes the side of Jesus
and is thus as a Christian bound to read the story in an anti-
Jewish sense. In a "prophetic reading" of the same text,
one takes the side of and identifies with the people of
Nazareth and thus is challenged by the word of Jesus.

> The two basic modes are the constitutive and the
> prophetic, according to context. The crucial distinc-
> tion between them is theological, the freedom of God
> on the one hand, and his [sic] generosity and grace on
> the other; and his [sic] apparent bias for the power-
> less, those who have not yet confused his [sic] power
> with theirs.[89]

The challenge of liberation theologies to the self-understanding of biblical scholarship can be supported by reference to recent epistemological discussions among historians and literary critics. A critical feminist biblical interpre-

tation therefore enhances rather than obstructs historical-critical scholarship. In my book *In Memory of Her: A Feminist Theological Reconstruction of Christian Origins*, I have sought to demonstrate how this is the case. Insofar as androcentric—male-centered—scholarship does not sufficiently take seriously the ideological character of androcentric texts and language, it cannot do justice to its sources. Insofar as this mode of scholarship presupposes an androcentric-patriarchal model for reconstructing early Christian origins without critically reflecting upon it, it cannot do justice to those texts that mention the leadership of women. More importantly, androcentric scholarship obscures the early Christian vision of the discipleship of equals and of the community embodying the new creation. Finally, insofar as it does not reflect critically on its own societal interests and ecclesiastical commitments, it cannot evaluate the significance and validity of biblical texts for women, who constitute, usually, the majority of the membership in biblical communities today.

A new critical self-understanding of biblical scholarship must lead to a new hermeneutic, not one of consent, but a hermeneutic of critical solidarity that can preserve the historical distance between the present and the past and at the same time share the faithful "memory" and the liberating visions of the past for the future. A new critical hermeneutics does not center on the text but on the people whose story with God is remembered in the texts of the Bible. Or, as James Barr has so succinctly stated, "The true believer is a believer in God and in Christ, not in the first place a believer in the Bible."[90] In this theological hermeneutics the biblical canon becomes the "prime paradigm" (J. Barr), the "paradigm of the verbs of God's activity" (J. Sanders), the "root-model" of Christian faith and practice (E. Schüssler Fiorenza), rather than the unchangeable "archetype" or the "magic Word" (A. C. Thiselton). If the process of inspiration is located in the history of God's people, then it is historical in character. But this history is not closed, it is ongoing, and it looks to the future of liberation and salvation for all humanity. This "future direction of Scripture," in Barr's terms, is of fundamental importance for the believing community on its way with God through history. The story of Sarah or the story of the Syrophoenician woman were not so much told to record what "actually happened" but to encourage us in the present and to furnish visions of an open future. Because of the critical and future-oriented dimensions of biblical scholarship as "interpretation for" the church of women, a critical feminist hermeneutics of liberation must have a fourfold dimension, as discussed in chapter 1. It must be a hermeneutics of suspicion, critically entering the biblical worlds and the works of scholars in order to detect their ideological deformations; a hermeneutics of remembrance, facilitated by literary and historical critical reconstructions; a hermeneutics of proclamation critically evaluating what can be proclaimed and taught today as an inspired vision for a more human life and future; and finally a hermeneutics of actualization that celebrates its critical solidarity in story and song, in ritual and meditation, as a people of the "God with us" who was the God of Judith as well as of Jesus.

We find signs today that biblical scholarship takes the challenge of liberation theologians seriously and that it is in the process of reconceptualizing its own understanding of history and interpretation. It can no longer articulate as its unqualified goal the intention to declare with scientific certainty what the text *meant*, because this is virtually an epistemological impossibility. Rather, it must seek to subject prevalent interpretations of what the text meant to a critical analysis, thereby testing for theological validity the self-understanding of social-ecclesial groups. Historical biblical consciousness is valuable not only as "anti-dogmatic weapon" but also as "a critical theological instrument for inquiring into the historical dimensions and social political ramifications of contemporary religious value-systems,"[91] as well as for challenging the theological self-understandings of contemporary Christians and church communities.

A renewed historical-critical self-understanding of biblical scholarship does not invite hermeneutical identification with biblical texts and historical practice—identification that obliterates the historical strangeness of the text—but historical solidarity with the people of God in biblical history.[92] It does not reconstruct biblical history as mirror image of our own society and church, but seeks to become a critical memory and theological-prophetic challenge to establishment society and church. Studying the biblical past to recover its unfulfilled historical possibilities and mandates thus becomes a primary task for biblical scholarship. It enables us to keep our future "open" in light of our biblical heritage and communal identity. It allows us to integrate biblical history and theology as a historical-theological biblical rhetoric for the future of the world and thereby also for the future of the Church. The new self-understanding of biblical scholarship as a critical historical-theological undertaking does not require detachment and neutrality but rather conversion and commitment to the biblical vision of humanity as the people of God. The common hermeneutical ground of past, present, and future is not "sacred history" or "sacred text" but commitment to the biblical vision of God's new creation.

Notes

Introduction

1. Alla Bozarth Campbell, *Womanpriest* (New York: Paulist Press, 198), pp. 217f.
2. Cynthia Ozick, "Notes toward Finding the Right Question," in Susan Heschel (ed.), *On Being a Jewish Feminist: A Reader* (New York: Schocken Books, 1983), p. 142.
3. Ibid., p. 144.
4. Judith Plaskow, "The Right Question Is Theological," in ibid., p. 231.
5. For the importance of Gage's thought see especially Sally Roesch Wagner, "Introduction," in Matilda Joslyn Gage, *Woman, Church, and State* (Watertown, Mass.: Persephone Press, 1983), pp. xv-xxxix.
6. Cf. the helpful review and discussion of different theological models of revelation (especially chapter 12, "The Bible: Document of Revelation") in Avery Dulles, *Models of Revelation* (Garden City, N.Y.: Doubleday, 1983). Dulles only mentions but does not elaborate the model of liberation theology, and does not consider the paradigm of feminist theology.
7. Cf. Dale Spender, *Man-Made Language* (London and Boston: Routledge and Kegan Paul, 1980), p. 150.
8. Elizabeth Cady Stanton (ed.), *The Original Feminist Attack on the Bible: The Woman's Bible* (1895; New York: Arno Press, 1974), with Barbara Welter's introduction.
9. Cf. especially Susan Brooks Thistlewaite, "Opening the Mail Which Did Not Tick," *Review of Books and Religion* 12/6 (1984): 6-8.
10. James J. Kilpatrick, "God Is Not a Chairperson," *Washington Post* (October 21, 1983). Positively, the *Inclusive Language Lectionary* has rekindled interest in textual criticism and biblical translation.
11. Angelina E. Grimké, "An Appeal to the Christian Women of the South," *Anti-Slavery Examiner* I/2 (1836): 16-26, argued that in God's eyes slavery was sin and the laws keeping slaves in bondage were man-made. Because of the attacks of the press and the clergy against them as women who spoke up, both Grimké sisters were drawn more deeply into the struggle for

women's rights. One of the signs is Sarah Grimké, *Letters on the Equality of the Sexes and the Condition of Women* (Boston: Isaac Knapp, 1838). Cf. Judith A. Sabrosky, *From Rationality to Liberation: The Evolution of Feminist Ideology* (Westport, Conn.: Greenwood Press, 1979). See also the review of opposing interpretations of the slave and women passages in the New Testament by Willard Swartley, *Slavery, Sabbath, War, and Women: Case Studies in Biblical Interpretation* (Philadelphia: Herald Press, 1983).

12. Cf. Charlene Spretnak, "The Christian Right's 'Holy War' against Feminism," in *The Politics of Women's Spirituality* (Garden City, N.Y.: Doubleday, Anchor Books, 1982), pp. 470-496; Shirley Rogers Radl, *The Invisible Woman: Target of the Religious Right* (New York: Delta Books, 1983).

13. See for instance my discussion of "the defense of Paul" in *In Memory of Her: A Feminist Theological Reconstruction of Christian Origins* (New York: Crossroad, 1983), pp. 8-10, and the theological rationalizations of the household code texts discussed in chapter 7, pp. 251-284.

14. This expression is taken from Judy Chicago, *The Dinner Party: A Symbol of Our Heritage* (Garden City, N.Y.: Doubleday, Anchor Books, 1979). See also Gustavo Gutierrez, *The Power of the Poor in History: Selected Writings* (Maryknoll, N.Y.: Orbis Press, 1983), especially chapter 7, "Theology from the Underside of History."

15. Cf. Andrea Dworkin, "Antifeminism," *Trivia* 2 (1983): 6-36, who concludes her analysis with this question: "Can a political movement rooted in a closed system—with no support among power-based movements—break that closed system apart? Or will the antifeminism of those whose politics are rooted in sex-class power and privilege always destroy movements for the liberation of women? Is there a way to subvert the antifeminism of power-based political programs or parties—or is the pleasure and profit in the subordination of women simply too overwhelming, too great, too marvelous to allow for anything but the political defense of that subordination (antifeminism)?" It is my contention here that a critical feminist interpretation of the Bible can contribute to such a "subversion of antifeminism" by denying any divine-religious authority to the biblical "subordination" passages and by "envisioning" and "building up" women-church as the discipleship community of equals that from "within" will contribute to break open the closed patriachal systems of church and society.

16. I have borrowed this expression from Marie Augusta Neal, although she uses it in a different context and sense. Cf. her *A*

Socio-Theology of Letting Go (New York: Paulist Press, 1977).
17. Adrienne Rich, "Disloyal to Civilization: Feminism, Racism, Gynephobia (1978)," in *On Lies, Secrets, and Silence* (New York: Norton, 1979), p. 307.
18. Notozake Shange's ending chorus *For Colored Girls Who Have Considered Suicide When the Rainbow Is Enuf* is often quoted by religious feminists. But it must not be overlooked that such an affirmation is only possible through the naming of sexist-racist oppressions. Anne Cameron, *Daughters of Copper Woman* (Vancouver: Press Gang Publishers, 1981), ends her record of stories about a secret society of native Vancouver Island women with a poem that concludes in a similar vein: "I have been searching Old Woman and I find her in mySelf" (p. 150).
19. Marcia Westkott, "Women's Studies as a Strategy for Change: Between Criticism and Vision," in Gloria Bowles and Renate Duelli Klein (eds.), *Theories of Women's Studies* (London and Boston: Routledge and Kegan Paul, 1983), p. 213.
20. Cf. for example Anne Carr, "Is a Christian Feminist Theology Possible?," *Theological Studies* 43 (1982): 279-297, and now also Rosemary Radford Ruether, "Feminist Interpretation: A Method of Correlation," in L. Russell (ed.), *Feminist Interpretation of the Bible* (Philadelphia: Westminster Press, forthcoming). For a discussion of such a method of correlation in contemporary theology see David Tracy, "Particular Questions with General Concerns," in Leonard Swidler (ed.), *Consensus in Theology* (Philadelphia: Westminster Press, 1980), pp. 33-39, and for a critical evaluation see Francis Schüssler Fiorenza, *Foundational Theology: Jesus and the Church* (New York: Crossroad, 1984), pp. 276-284.
21. My position is often misunderstood as postulating a period of equality in the earliest beginnings of the church, which very soon was superseded by the patriarchal form of church. My point, however, is not only that the "discipleship of equals" preceded the "patriarchalization" of church but also that it was repressed rather than replaced. Although the discipleship community of equals or women-church was submerged and often oppressed by ecclesiastical patriarchy, it has never ceased to exist. Rather than conceptualize church history as a history of decline (or progress, depending on the point of view), I conceptualize it as a history of struggle. Insofar as the Bible is the model for both women-church *and* patriarchal church, it is also the paradigm of this struggle.
22. Mary Ann Tolbert, "Defining the Problem: The Bible and Feminist Hermeneutics," in *Semeia: The Bible and Feminist Hermeneutics* 28 (1983): 123, seems to assume that I propose a

reconstruction of the earliest egalitarian period of early Christianity as the basis of faith. I hope it has become clear that this is not the case. Although I share Bultmann's program of *Sachkritik*, I do not share his neo-orthodox existentialist position or his method of demythologization. I completely agree with Tolbert that the biblical texts cannot be "depatriarchalized" (in analogy to demythologized). At the same time I cannot accept the first part of Tolbert's suggestion that a feminist hermeneutics must seek "to understand the same God as enemy and friend, as tormentor and savior." Her additional phrase "to read the same Bible as enslaver and liberator, that is the paradoxical challenge of feminist biblical hermeneutics" (p. 126) restates my own position. My argument has been precisely that God and the Bible cannot be commensurate if we take the feminist hermeneutical insight seriously that the Bible is "man-made," written in androcentric language and rooted in patriarchal cultures and religions.

23. In lectures and conversations, Mary Elizabeth Hunt first has suggested this analogy between math anxiety and theology anxiety.

24. Dorothy Smith, "A Peculiar Eclipsing: Women's Exclusion from Man's Culture," *Women's Studies International Quarterly* I/4 (1978): 281.

25. Dale Spender, *Women of Ideas and What Men Have Done to Them: From Aphra Behn to Adrienne Rich* (London: ARK Paperbacks, 1982), p. 8.

26. See especially the influential contribution of Nelle Morton, "The Rising Women's Consciousness in a Male Language Structure," in *Women and the Word: Toward a Whole Theology* (Berkeley: GTU, 1972), pp. 43–52.

27. See Letty M. Russell, *Feminist Interpretation of the Bible* (Philadelphia: Westminster Press, forthcoming).

28. This is underlined in Beverly Wildung Harrison's reflections on my book in "Review Symposium: *In Memory of Her: Four Perspectives,*" *Horizons* 11 (1984), pp. 140–157.

29. Richard J. Bernstein, *Beyond Objectivism and Relativism: Science, Hermeneutics, and Praxis* (Philadelphia: University of Pennsylvania Press, 1983), p. 231.

30. The "true" answer to this question cannot be substantiated by hermeneutic-theological theory but must be validated in the emancipatory praxis of women-church. Feminist theology is a second-order reflection.

31. Renny Golden and Sheila Collins, *Struggle Is a Name for Hope: Poetry*, Worker Writer Series 3 (Minneapolis, 1983), p. 20.

1. Women-Church

1. See chapter 4.
2. As quoted in Bell Hooks, *Ain't I a Woman: Black Women and Feminism* (Boston: South End Press, 1981), pp. 193f.
3. Elizabeth Cady Stanton (ed.), *The Original Feminist Attack on the Bible: The Woman's Bible* (1895; New York: Arno Press, 1974), p. 7.
4. Rosemary Radford Ruether, "Feminism and Patriarchal Religion: Principles of Ideological Critique of the Bible," *Journal for the Study of the Old Testament* 22 (1982): 54-66.
5. Letty Russell, "Feminist Critique: Opportunity for Cooperation," *Journal for the Study of the Old Testament* 22 (1982): 68.
6. See chapter 2.
7. See the review article by R. S. Kraemer, "Women in the Religions of the Greco-Roman World," *Religious Studies Review* 9 (1983): 127-139, for an extensive discussion of historical-critical studies.
8. See Johann Baptist Metz, *Faith in History and Society: Toward a Practical Fundamental Theology*, trans. David Smith (New York: Crossroad, 1980).

2. 'For the Sake of Our Salvation . . .'

1. For the literature on the scholarly discussion of this problem, see especially Peter Stuhlmacher, *Historical Criticism and Theological Interpretation of Scripture: Toward a Hermeneutics of Consent* (Philadelphia: Fortress Press, 1977); E. Krentz, *The Historical-Critical Method* (Philadelphia: Fortress Press, 1975), especially pp. 55-58; D. H. Kelsey, *The Uses of Scripture in Recent Theology* (Philadelphia: Fortress Press, 1975); Walter Wink, *The Bible in Human Transformation: Toward a New Paradigm for Biblical Study* (Philadelphia: Fortress Press, 1973).
2. Thomas S. Kuhn, *The Structure of Scientific Revolutions* (Chicago: University of Chicago Press, 1962); Ian G. Barbour, *Myth, Models, and Paradigms,* (New York: Harper and Row, 1974).
3. See R. Grant, *The Bible in the Church: A Short History of Interpretation,* rev. ed. (New York: Macmillan, 1963); H. J. Kraus, *Geschichte der historisch-kritischen Erforschung des Alten Testaments* (Neukirchen: Neukirchener Verlag, 1969); R. E. Clements, *One Hundred Years of Old New Testament Interpretation* (Philadelphia: Westminster Press, 1976); W. G. Kümmel, *The New Testament: The History of the Investigation of*

Its Problems (Nashville: Abingdon, 1972).

4. See the excellent analysis of J. Barr, *Fundamentalism* (Philadelphia: Westminster Press, 1978).

5. See text and analysis in L. Swidler and A. Swidler (eds.), *Women Priests: A Catholic Commentary on the Vatican Declaration* (New York: Paulist Press, 1977), and C. Stuhlmueller (ed.), *Women and Priesthood: Future Directions* (Collegeville, Minn.: Liturgical Press, 1978). For the strained relationship between exegesis and dogmatics, see J. L. Houlden, *Patterns of Faith: A Study in the Relationship between the New Testament and Christian Doctrine* (Philadelphia: Fortress Press, 1977).

6. See my book *Priester für Gott: Studien zum Herrschafts-und Priesterbegriff in der Apokalypse*, Neutestamentliche Abhandlungen 7 (Münster: Aschendorff Verlag, 1972), and my article "Cultic Language in Qumran and in the New Testament," *CBQ* 38 (1976): 159-177, for the literature.

7. See the articles of A. Smitmans and H. Harsch, in H. Harsch and G. Voss (eds.), *Versuche mehrdimensionaler Schriftauslegung* (Stuttgart: Verlag Katholisches Bibelwerk, 1972).

8. Wink, *The Bible in Human Transformation*, pp. 56f.

9. See C. K. Barrett, *Biblical Problems and Biblical Preaching*, Biblical Series 6 (Philadelphia: Fortress Press, 1964), p. 37.

10. See P. Stuhlmacher, *Historical Criticism*, p. 36.

11. See J. Barr, *Fundamentalism*, p. 312: "This is one of the main features in the fundamentalist mind: The fact that a man says he believes in Christ does not seem objective to them, you can't trust that or rely on it, but if he believes in the Bible as infallible and inerrant then that seems to lend objectivity. Objectivity thus comes to mean that the truth is not in people."

12. T. A. Collins and R. E. Brown, "Church Pronouncements," *JBC* II (1968): 624-632.

13. "Difficulties in Using the New Testament in American Catholic Discussion," *Louvain Studies* 6 (1976): 144-158.

14. See K. Stendahl, "Biblical Theology, Contemporary," *The Interpreter's Dictionary of the Bible*, vol. 1 (Nashville: Abingdon, 1962), 418-432 (hereafter cited as *IDB*), and F. Hahn, "Probleme historischer Kritik," *ZNTW* 63 (1972): 1-17.

15. Lonergan's eight functional specialties in theology are often understood in such a way. See his *Method in Theology* (New York: Herder and Herder, 1972).

16. I understand *pastoral* here not in the sense of a theology for pastors or ministers but in the sense of a theology pertaining to the community of faith. Most discussions on biblical preaching see the problem too narrowly as one concerned with pastors

or preachers.

17. See N. Perrin, *What is Redaction Criticism?* (Philadelphia: Fortress Press, 1976); J. Rohde, *Rediscovering the Teachings of the Evangelists* (Philadelphia: Westminster Press, 1969); J. Reumann, "Methods in Studying the Biblical Text Today," *Concordia Theological Monthly* 40 (1969): 655-681; W. G. Kümmel, *Das Neue Testament im 20. Jahrhundert,* Stuttgarter Bibelstudien 50 (Stuttgart: Verlag Katholisches Bibelwerk, 1970).

18. For a review of the hermeneutical discusssion, see R. E. Brown, "Hermeneutics," *JBC* II (1968): 605-623, and J. A. Sanders, "Hermeneutics," *IDB* (suppl. vol. 1976): 402-407.

19. See J. Habermas, "Der Universalitätsanspruch der Hermeneutik," in *Kultur und Kritik* (Frankfurt, 1973), pp. 264-301, and the theological work of Francis Schüssler Fiorenza; see also my article "Feminist Theology as a Critical Theology of Liberation," *Theological Studies* 36 (1975): 605-626.

20. See L. E. Keck, *The New Testament Experience of Faith* (St. Louis: Bethany Press, 1976), and his article "On the Ethos of Early Christians," *JAAR* 42 (1974): 435-452.

21. See V. Furnish, *The Love Command in the New Testament* (Nashville: Abingdon, 1972).

22. See *Aspects of Religious Propaganda in Judaism and Early Christianity* (Notre Dame, Ind.: Notre Dame University Press, 1976), which I edited.

23. See John C. Gager, *Kingdom and Community: The Social World of Early Christianity* (Englewood Cliffs, N.J.: Prentice-Hall, 1975); N. K. Gottwald and F. S. Frick, "The Social World of Ancient Israel," in *The Bible and Liberation* (Berkeley, Calif.: Radical Religion Reader, 1976), pp. 110-119; G. Theissen, *Sociology of Early Palestinian Christianity* (Philadelphia: Fortress Press, 1978); W. A. Meeks, "The Social World of Early Christianity," *CSR Bulletin* 6 (1975): 1, 4f.

24. See Perrin, *What Is Redaction Criticism?*, pp. 76f.

25. Sanders, "Hermeneutics," pp. 406f., advocates the rule of "dynamic analogy" for such a translation and distinguishes the constitutive and prophetic mode of interpretation.

26. For a discussion of the problem see Jean Charlot, *New Testament Disunity: Its Significance for Christianity Today* (New York: E. P. Dutton, 1970), and E. Krentz, "A Survey of Trends and Problems in Biblical Interpretation," *Concordia Theological Monthly* 40 (1969): 276-293.

27. See R. Mackenzie, "The Self-Understanding of the Exegete," in R. Murphy (ed.), *Theology, Exegesis, and Proclamation,* Concilium Series 70 (New York: Herder and Herder, 1971), pp. 11-

19; R. L. Rohrbaugh, *The Biblical Interpreter* (Philadelphia: Fortress Press, 1978).

28. See E. Schillebeeckx, *The Understanding of Faith* (New York: Seabury, 1974).

29. See T. Peters, "The Nature and Role of Presuppositions: An Inquiry into Contemporary Hermeneutics, *International Philosophical Quarterly* 14 (1974): 209-222.

30. See F. Herzog, "Liberation Hermeneutics as Ideology Critique," *Interpretation* 27 (1974): 387-403.

31. This is especially emphasized by liberation theology. See the article of Lee Cormie, "The Hermeneutical Privilege of the Oppressed," Proceedings of the CTSA 32 (1978): 155-181, and the review article by J. A. Kirk, "The Bible in Latin American Liberation Theology," in N. Gottwald and A. Wire (eds.), *The Bible and Liberation* (Berkeley, Calif.: Radical Religion Reader, 1976): 157-165.

32. See the very interesting report of J. Rothermund, "Laien als Partner in der Predigtarbeit," *Wissenschaft und Praxis in Kirche und Gesellschaft* 67 (1978): 187-201; and especially the two volumes edited by E. Cardenal, *The Gospel in Solentiname* (Maryknoll, N.Y.: Orbis Books, 1976).

33. Stuhlmacher, *Historical Criticism*, pp. 83ff., has coined this expression. In a "hermeneutics of consent" we must not only ask how we relate to the text. "But in addition we must again learn to ask what claim or truth about man, his world, and transcendence we hear from these texts" (p. 85).

34. See E. Käsemann, "The Canon of the New Testament and the Unity of the Church," in *Essays on New Testament Themes* (London: SCM Press, 1964); and Charlot, *New Testament Disunity*, pp. 39-94.

35. See J. C. Turro and R. E. Brown, "Canonicity," *JBC* II (1968): 514-534, especially pp. 532ff.

36. For such a proposal see S. M. Ogden, "The Authority of Scripture for Theology," *Interpretation* 30 (1976): 242-261, who follows W. Marxsen.

37. W. Abbott and J. Gallagher (eds.), *The Documents of Vatican II* (New York: America Press, 1966), p. 108.

38. Ibid., p. 119.

39. See also my "Understanding God's Revealed Word," in *Catholic Charismatic* 1 (1977): 4-10, and "Interpreting Patriarchal Traditions of the Bible," in Letty Russell (ed.), *The Liberating Word: A Guide to Nonsexist Interpretation of the Bible* (Philadelphia: Westminster Press, 1976): 39-61.

3. The Function of Scripture in the Liberation Struggle

1. See Adrienne Rich, "Toward a Woman-Centered University," in

Florence Howe (ed.), *Women and the Power to Change* (New York: McGraw-Hill, 1975): 15-46; and my analysis in "Toward a Liberating and Liberated Theology: Women Theologians and Feminist Theology in the U.S.A.," *Concilium* 115 (1979): 22-32.

2. See for example Lisa Leghorn and M. Roodkowsky, *Who Really Starves? Women and World Hunger* (New York: Friendship Press, 1977); Diane E. Nichole Russel and N. Van de Ven (eds.), *Crimes against Women: Proceedings of the International Tribunal* (Millbrae, Calif.: Les Femmes, 1976); Susan Hill Lindley, "Feminist Theology in a Global Perspective," *Christian Century* 96 (April 25, 1979): 465-469.

3. See, for instance, Gustavo Gutierrez, *A Theology of Liberation* (Maryknoll, N.Y.: Orbis Books, 1973), pp. 204-205: "A spirituality of liberation will center on a *conversion* to the neighbor, the oppressed person, the exploited social class, the despised race, the dominated country. Our conversion to the Lord implies this conversion to the neighbor." Compare the description of feminist conversion by Judith Plaskow, *Sex, Sin, and Grace: Women's Experience and the Theologies of Reinhold Niebuhr and Paul Tillich* (Washington, D.C.: University Press of America, 1980), pp. 171-172: "The woman who, having seen the nonbeing of social structures, feels herself a whole person, is called upon to become the person she is in that movement. . . . The experience of grace is not the experience of the sole activity of God, but the experience of the emergence of the 'I' as cocreator. . . . Relatedness to God is expressed through the never-ending journey toward self-creation with community, and through the creation of ever wider communities, including both other human beings and the world."

4. Robert McAfee Brown, *Theology in a New Key: Responding to Liberation Themes* (Philadelphia: Westminster Press, 1978), p. 82.

5. Vine Deloria, "A Native American Perspective on Liberation," in *Mission Trends* No. 4; *Liberation Theologies*, Gerald H. Anderson and Thomas F. Stransky (eds.), (New York: Paulist Press, 1979), pp. 261-270.

6. See my "Women in Early Christianity: Methodological Considerations," in T. J. Ryan (ed.), *Critical History and Biblical Faith in New Testament Perspectives* (Villanova, Pa.: Catholic Theology Society Annual Publications, 1979), pp. 30-58.

7. See chapter 2 for an extensive discussion of the literature.

8. See Lee Cormie, "The Hermeneutical Privilege of the Oppressed: Liberation Theologies, Biblical Faith, and Marxist Sociology of Knowledge," *Proceedings of the Catholic Theological Society of America* 32 (1978): 155-181; D. Lockhead, "Hermeneutics and Ideology," *Ecumenist* 15 (1977): 81-84.

160 • BREAD NOT STONE

9. Schubert M. Ogden, *Faith and Freedom: Toward a Theology of Liberation* (Nashville: Abingdon, 1979), p. 116.
10. Ibid., p. 32.
11. James H. Cone, *God of the Oppressed* (New York: Seabury, 1975), pp. 51-52.
12. See Charles H. Strain, "Ideology and Alienation: Theses on the Interpretation and Evaluation of Theologies of Liberation," *JAAR* 45 (1977): 474.
13. See Thomas S. Kuhn, *The Structure of Scientific Revolutions* (Chicago: University of Chicago Press, 1962); Ian G. Barbour, *Myth, Models, and Paradigms* (New York: Harper and Row, 1974).
14. See chapter 2 for the development of these paradigms. See also for the general paradigm shift in biblical studies, Walter Wink, *The Bible in Human Transformation: Toward a New Paradigm for Biblical Study* (Philadelphia: Fortress Press, 1973).
15. See especially Peter Stuhlmacher, *Historical Criticism and Theological Interpretation of Scripture: Toward a Hermeneutics of Consent* (Philadelphia: Fortress Press, 1977), pp. 38ff.
16. For these criteria, see Ogden, *Faith and Freedom*, p. 26, and especially David Tracy, *Blessed Rage for Order: The New Pluralism in Theology* (New York: Seabury, 1975), pp. 72-79.
17. This whole section is based on an analysis of Juan Luis Segundo, *The Liberation of Theology* (Maryknoll, N.Y.: Orbis Books, 1976).
18. Ibid., p. 9; see also Jose Miguez Bonino, *Doing Theology in a Revolutionary Situation* (Philadelphia: Fortress Press, 1975), pp. 86-105, who accepts Professor Casalis's reformulation of the "hermeneutical circle" as "hermeneutical circulation" (p. 102).
19. Segundo, *The Liberation of Theology*, p. 8.
20. Ibid., p. 110.
21. Ibid., p. 179.
22. See my "Feminist Spirituality, Christian Identity, and the Catholic Vision," in Carol P. Christ and Judith Plaskow (eds.), *Womanspirit Rising: A Feminist Reader in Religion* (New York: Harper and Row, 1979). pp. 136-148.
23. Elizabeth Cady Stanton (ed.), *The Original Feminist Attack on the Bible: The Woman's Bible* (1895; New York: Arno Press, 1974).
24. Barbara Welter, "Something Remains to Dare," introduction to Cady Stanton, *The Woman's Bible*, p. xxii.
25. Cady Stanton, *The Woman's Bible*, 1:9.
26. Ibid., II:7f.
27. Ibid., I:12.

28. See, however, Marie Fortune and Joann Haugerud, *Study Guide to the Woman's Bible* (Seattle: Coalition Task Force on Women and Religion, 1975), for a contemporary application; and Leonard Swidler, *Biblical Affirmations of Woman* (Philadelphia: Westminster Press, 1979), who basically follows the same principle.
29. Cited in Cady Stanton, *The Woman's Bible*, II:200.
30. Gustavo Gutierrez, "Where Hunger Is, God Is Not," *Witness* 59 (April 1976): 6.
31. For the conceptualization of feminist theology as a critical theology of liberation, see my "Feminist Theology as a Critical Theology of Liberation," in Walter Burkhardt (ed.), *Woman: New Dimensions* (New York: Paulist Press, 1977), pp. 19–50.
32. See the path-breaking article of Francis Schüssler Fiorenza, "Critical Social Theology and Christology: Toward an Understanding of Atonement and Redemption as Emancipatory Solidarity," *Proceedings of the Catholic Theological Society of America* 30 (1975): 63–110.
33. Ogden, *Faith and Freedom*, pp. 44ff., and his article, "The Authority of Scripture for Theology, *Interpretation* 30 (1976): 242–261.
34. For the expression, *"norma...,"* see David Tracy, "Theological Classics in Contemporary Theology," *Theology Digest* 25 (1977): 347–355.
35. James H. Cone, *Liberation: A Black Theology of Liberation* (Philadelphia: Lippincott, 1970), p. 80.
36. Jon Sobrino, "The Historical Jesus and the Christ of Faith," *Cross Currents* 27 (1977/78): 437–463, 460.
37. This proposal should not be understood in the sense of the approach taken by *The Woman's Bible*, which singled out for discussion biblical texts on women. The criterion has to be applied to all biblical texts insofar as they claim authority for today. Such a theological evaluation must also be distinguished from a reconstruction of early Christian history in a feminist perspective. While a feminist reconstruction of early Christian history seeks women's history and heritage, a feminist biblical hermeneutics evaluates the claims to truth of biblical texts for today. Thus both approaches are interdependent but quite distinct.
38. See my analysis in "Word, Spirit, and Power: Women in Early Christian Communities," in Rosemary R. Ruether and Eleanor McLaughlin (eds.), *Women of Spirit* (New York: Simon and Schuster, 1979), pp. 29–70.
39. Rachel Blau DuPlessis, "The Critique of Consciousness and Myth in Levertov, Rich, and Rukeyser," *Feminist Studies* 3 (1975): 199–221, 219.

40. Rosemary Radford Ruether, *New Woman/New Earth: Sexist Ideologies and Human Liberation* (New York: Seabury, 1975), pp. 115-132, has called for an "interstructuring" of various models of alienation and liberation.

4. **Discipleship and Patriarchy**

1. For a review and discussion of the hermeneutical and methodological issues involved see among others E. LeRoy Long, Jr., "The Use of the Bible in Christian Ethics: A Look at Basic Options," *Interpretation* 9 (1965): 149-162; Charles Curran, "Dialogue with the Scriptures: The Role and Function of the Scriptures in Moral Deliberation and Justification," in *Catholic Moral Theology in Dialogue* (Notre Dame, Ind.: Fides Publishers, 1972), pp. 24-64; James M. Gustafson, "The Place of Scripture in Christian Ethics: A Methodological Study," *Interpretation* 24 (1970): 430-455; Allen Verhey, "The Use of Scripture in Ethics," *Religious Studies Review* 4 (1978): 28-39; James Childress, "Scripture and Christian Ethics: Some Reflections on the Role of Scripture in Moral Deliberation and Justification," *Interpretation* 34 (1980): 371-380; and the very useful book of Bruce C. Birch and Larry L. Rasmussen, *Bible and Ethics in the Christian Life* (Minneapolis: Augsburg Publishing House, 1976).

2. Stanley Hauerwas, "The Moral Authority of Scripture: The Politics and Ethics of Remembering," *Interpretation* 34 (1980): 356-370, 367.

3. See for example Bernhard Fraling, "Glaube und Ethos: Normfindung in der Gemeinschaft der Gläubigen," *Theologie und Glaube* 63 (1973); 81-105, and the diverse writings of James Barr, especially his contribution "The Bible as Document of Believing Communities," in Hans Dieter Betz (ed.), *The Bible as a Document of the University* (Chico, Calif.: Scholars Press, 1981), pp. 25-47.

4. For a discussion of different paradigms and heuristic models in biblical interpretation see chapter 2.

5. For a helpful review of the problem see Jean Charlot, *New Testament Disunity: Its Significance for Christianity Today* (New York: E. P. Dutton, 1970).

6. For the definition of ethics as "an evaluative hermeneutics of history" see Gibson Winter, *Elements for a Social Ethics: Scientific and Ethical Perspectives on Social Process* (New York: Macmillan, 1966), and Thomas W. Ogletree, "The Activity of Interpreting in Moral Judgment," *Journal of Religious Ethics* 8 (1980): 1-25. Ogletree proposes a "historical style" in ethics as an "explication of meanings forming the life worlds of representative actors in concrete situations."

7. See Johann Baptist Metz, *Faith in History and Society: Toward a Practical Fundamental Theology*, trans. David Smith (New York: Crossroad, 1980), pp. 88-118, 185-199.

8. For this expression see "The Constitution on Divine Revelation of Vatican II." in Walter Abbott and Joseph Gallagher (eds.), *The Documents of Vatican II* (New York: America Press, 1966), p. 119. Salvation must not be restricted to the salvation of the soul from sin, but must be understood as total human wholeness and liberation.

9. Hauerwas, "The Moral Authority of Scripture," p. 356. Like Metz, Hauerwas uses as key interpretive categories memory and narrative/story, but neglects how Metz spells out their critical implications. Insofar as Hauerwas asserts that the church is the "community of the forgiven" without asking it to repent and to reject its oppressive traditions, he does not do justice to the memory of the innocent victims in history. Thus his theology has no room for a critical hermeneutics of liberation.

10. Elizabeth Cady Stanton, *The Original Feminist Attack on the Bible: The Woman's Bible* (New York: Arno Press, 1974), p. 7.

11. See Linda Gordon and Allen Hunter, "Sex, Family, and the New Right: Antifeminism as a Political Force," *Radical America* 11 (1978): 9-25; Charlene Spretnak, "The Christian Right's 'Holy War' against Feminism," in *The Politics of Women's Spirituality* (Garden City, N.Y.: Doubleday, Anchor Books, 1982), pp. 470-496.

12. See my article "'You Are Not to Be Called Father': Early Christian History in a Feminist Perspective," *Cross Currents* 39 (1979): 301-323, for a methodological discussion of these dynamics.

13. David L. Balch, *Let Wives Be Submissive: The Domestic Code in 1 Peter*, SBL Monograph Series 36 (Chico, Calif.: Scholars Press, 1981).

14. Stephen B. Clark, *Man and Woman in Christ: An Examination of the Roles of Men and Women in Light of Scripture and the Social Sciences* (Ann Arbor, Mich.: Servant Books, 1980).

15. John H. Elliott, *A Home for the Homeless: A Sociological Exegesis of I Peter, Its Situation and Strategy* (Philadelphia: Fortress Press, 1981).

16. Karl Niederwimmer, *Askese und Mysterium*, FRLANT 113 (Göttingen: Vandenhoeck and Ruprecht, 1975).

17. James E. Crouch, *The Origins and Intention of the Colossian Haustafel*, FRLANT 109 (Göttingen: Vandenhoeck and Ruprecht, 1972).

18. Klaus Thraede, "Frau," *Antike und Christentum* 6 (1970): 197-267.

164 • BREAD NOT STONE

19. William Lillie, "The Pauline House-Tables," *Expository Times* 86 (1975): 179-182, acknowledges the "pattern of submission" as characteristic for the household code texts. For a christological justification of this pattern of subordination see Else Kähler, *Die Frau in den Paulinischen Briefen* (Zurich: Gotthelf Verlag, 1960). For a feminist evangelical interpretation of the pattern as a pattern of "mutual submission" see Virginia Ramey Mollenkott, *Women, Men, and the Bible* (Nashville: Abingdon, 1977), and Letha Scanzoni and Nancy Hardesty, *All We're Meant to Be: A Biblical Approach to Women's Liberation* (Waco; Texas: Word Books, 1975).
20. For a review of the discussion see Ulrich Luz, "Erwägungen zur Entstehung des 'Frühkatholizismus'," *Zeitschrift für die Neutestamentliche Wissenschaft* 65 (1974): 88-111.
21. Dieter Lührmann, "Wo man nicht mehr Sklave und Freier ist: Überlegungen zur Struktur frühchristlicher Gemeinden," *Wort und Dienst* 13 (1975): 53-83.
22. Ronald Syme, *The Roman Revolution* (Oxford: Oxford University Press, 1939), pp. 509-524.
23. Among others see David Schroeder, "Die Haustafeln des Neuen Testaments" (Ph.D. diss., University of Hamburg, 1959), whose thesis was popularized in English by John H. Yoder.
24. For a review of this position and its main representatives see the works of Crouch, Balch, and Elliott.
25. See Klaus Thraede, "Zum historischen Hintergrund der 'Haustafeln' des NT," *Jahrbuch für Antike und Christentum, Ergänzungsband* 8 (1981): 359-368; Kahtleen O'Brien Wicker, "First Century Marriage Ethics: A Comparative Study of the Household Codes and Plutarch's Conjugal Precepts," in James Flanagan and Anita W. Robinson (eds.), *No Famine in the Land* (Missoula, Mon.: Scholars Press, 1975), pp. 141-153; David Balch, "Household Ethical Codes in Peripatetic, Neopythagorean, and Early Christian Moralists," in Paul J. Archtemeier (ed.), *Society of Biblical Literature Seminar Papers II* (Missoula, Mon.: Scholars Press, 1977), pp. 397-404.
26. See the following by Gerd Theissen: "Itinerant Radicalism: The Tradition of Jesus Sayings from the Perspective of the Sociology of Literature," in *The Bible and Liberation: Political and Social Hermeneutics* (Berkeley, Calif.: Radical Religion Reader, 1976), pp. 84-93; *Sociology of Early Palestinian Christianity* (Philadelphia: Fortress Press, 1978); and *The Social Setting of Pauline Christianity: Essays on Corinth* (Philadelphia: Fortress Press, 1982).
27. Elliott, *A Home for the Homeless*, p. 198.

28. See my "Word, Spirit, and Power: Women in Early Christian Communities," in Rosemary E. Ruether and Eleanor McLaughlin (eds.), *Women of Spirit* (New York: Simon and Schuster, 1979), pp. 29-70, and "Women in the Pre-Pauline and Pauline Churches," *Union Seminar Quarterly Review* 33 (1978): 153-166.

29. For an excellent discussion of the "slavery passages" see Peter Trummer, "Die Chance der Freiheit," *Biblica* 56 (1975): 344-368, and the commentaries to Philemon.

30. Robert A. Nisbet, *The Social Philosophers: Community and Conflict in Western Thought* (New York: Thomas Y. Cromwell, 1973), p. 178.

31. Edwin A. Judge, *The Social Patterns of Christian Groups in the First Century: Some Prolegomena to the Study of New Testament Ideas of Social Organization* (London: Tyndale, 1960), pp. 75f.

32. Ibid., p. 76.

33. For the distinction between ethos and ethics see Leander E. Keck, "Ethos and Ethics in the New Testament," in James Gaffney (ed.), *Essays in Morality and Ethics* (New York: Paulist Press, 1980), pp. 29-49. For the interrelation between house-church and collegia see Abraham Malherbe, *Social Aspects of Early Christianity* (Baton Rouge: Louisiana State University, 1977).

34. See Susan Treggiari, "Roman Social History: Recent Interpretations," *Histoire Social: Social History* 8 (1975): 149-164, and Wayne A. Meeks, "The Image of the Androgyne," *History of Religion* 13 (1974): 167-180, for a review of the literature.

35. Klaus Thraede, "Aerger mit der Freiheit: Die Bedeutung von Frauen in Theorie und Praxis der alten Kirche," in Gerda Scharffenroth (ed.), *Freunde in Christus werden...* (Gelnhausen and Berlin: Burckhardthaus, 1977), pp. 35-182.

36. See the discussion of the literature by Georg Strecker, "Strukturen einer neutestamentlichen Ethik," *Zeitschrift für Theologie und Kirche* 75 (1978): 117-146; Siegfried Schulz, "Evangelium und Welt: Hauptprobleme einer Ethik des Neuen Testaments," in Hans Dieter Betz and Luise Schottroff (eds.), *Neues Testament und christliche Existenz*, Festschrift H. Braun (Tübingen: JCB Mohr, 1973), pp. 483-501.

37. See John G. Gager, *Kingdom and Community: The Social World of Early Christianity* (Englewood Cliffs; N.J.: Prentice-Hall, 1975), and Gerd Theissen, "Itinerant Radicalism" (see n. 26), pp. 91f.

38. Eduard Schweizer, "Ethischer Pluralismus im Neuen Testament: Die Haustafeln," in *Beiträge zur alttestamentlichen*

Theologie, Festschrift W. Zimmerli (Göttingen: Vandenhoeck and Ruprecht, 1979), pp. 397-413, 412.

39. Leonhard Goppelt, *Der erste Petrusbrief,* ed. Ferdinand Hahn, Meyer Kommentor (Göttingen: Vandenhoeck and Ruprecht, 1978), pp. 163-177.

40. Wolfgang Schrage, "Zur Ethik der neutestamentlichen Haustafeln," *New Testament Studies* 21 (1974/75): 1-22, 22.

41. John Howard Yoder, *The Politics of Jesus: Vicit Agnus Noster* (Grand Rapids, Mich.: W. B. Eerdmans, 1972), p. 175.

42. Ibid., p. 185.

43. Ibid., p. 176 n. 22. See also "The Moral Authority of Scripture," p. 370.

44. See for example Mary Daly's feminist stance in *Beyond God the Father* (Boston: Beacon Press, 1973), which conceives of "sisterhood as anti-church," and in *Gyn/Ecology: The Metaethics of Radical Feminism* (Boston: Beacon Press, 1978), which redefines sisterhood in terms of "the bonding of the Selfs" who have "escaped" from patriarchal space as "the territory of nonbeing." This understanding of "sisterhood" no longer can sustain feminist solidarity with all women because it does not understand the feminist movement as the "bonding of the oppressed" but as the gathering of the ideologically "pure," as "the network of Spinsters and Amazons."

45. Elisabeth Schüssler Fiorenza, "Feminist Theology as a Critical Theology of Liberation," *Theological Studies* 36 (1975): 605-626; Carol S. Robb, "A Framework for Feminist Ethics," *Journal of Religious Ethics* 9 (1981): 48-68; and especially the very helpful introductions by Carol Christ and Judith Plaskow (eds.), *Womanspirit Rising: A Feminist Reader in Religion* (New York: Harper and Row, 1979).

46. See my articles, "Interpreting Patriarchal Traditions of the Bible," in Letty Russell (ed.), *The Liberating Word: A Guide to Nonsexist Interpretation of the Bible* (Philadelphia: Westminster Press, 1976), pp. 39-61, and chapter 3. See also Elizabeth Fox-Genovese, "For Feminist Interpretation," *Union Seminary Quarterly Review* 35 (1979/80): 5-14; Ernst Feil, "'Konfessorische' Implikationen der Wissenschaft: Folgerungen für die theologische Ethik," *Herder Korrespondenz* 34 (1980): 28-37.

47. For a similar but distinct approach see Beverly Wildung Harrison, "The Power of Anger in the Work of Love: Christian Ethics for Women and Other Strangers," *Union Seminary Quarterly Review* 36 (1981): 41-57; Eleanor Humes Haney, "What Is Feminist Ethics? A Proposal for Continuing Discussion," *Journal of Religious Ethics* 8 (1980): 115-124.

48. For this distinction see Letty Russell, *Human Liberation in a Feminist Perspective: A Theology* (Philadelphia: Westminster Press, 1974).
49. Phyllis Trible, *God and the Rhetoric of Sexuality* (Philadelphia: Fortress Press, 1978), uses the metaphor of the biblical text "wandering through history to merge past and present."
50. This position is succinctly stated by Rosemary Radford Ruether, "The Feminist Critique in Religious Studies," *Soundings* 64 (1981): 388-402, 400: "Liberationists would use the prophetic tradition as the norm to critique the sexism of the religious tradition. Biblical sexism is not denied, but it loses its authority. It must be denounced as a failure to measure up to the full vision of human liberation of the prophetic and gospel messages."
51. See my "Sexism and Conversion," *Network* 9 (1981): 12-22.
52. For this distinction between archetype and prototype see Rachel Blau DuPlessis, "The Critique of Consciousness and Myth in Levertov, Rich, and Rukeyser," *Feminist Studies* 3 (1975): 199-221.
53. Susan Moller Okin, *Women in Western Political Thought* (Princeton; N.J.: Princeton University Press, 1979), p. 276.
54. Ibid., p. 289. See also Nannerl O. Koehane, "Speaking from Silence: Women and the Science of Politics," *Soundings* 64 (1981): 422-436.
55. Okin, *Women in Western Political Thought*, p. 296.
56. See also Beverly Wildung Harrison, "Some Problems for Normative Christian Family Ethics," in *Selected Papers, 1977: The American Society of Christian Ethics* (Waterloo: Council on the Study of Religion, 1977), pp. 72-85; Barbara Hilkert Andolson, "Agape in Feminist Ethics," *Journal of Religious Ethics* 9 (1981): 69-81.

5. Remembering the Past in Creating the Future

1. G. Dautzenberg, H. Merklein, K. H. Müller (eds.), *Die Frau im Urchristentum*, Quaestiones Disputatae 95 (Freiburg: Herder, 1983). The preface does not mention that the conference as well as this collection of papers was an indirect response to my paper "Der Beitrag der Frau zur urchristlichen Bewegung: Kritische Überlegungen zur Rekonstruktion urchristlicher Geschichte," in W. Schottroff and W. Stegemann (eds.), *Traditionen der Befreiung, 2: Frauen in der Bibel* (Munich and Gelnhausen: Kaiser-/Burckardthaus Verlag, 1980), pp. 60-90.
2. See especially J. Neusner, *Method and Meaning in Ancient Judaism*, Brown Judaic Studies 10 (Missoula, Mon.: Scholars Press, 1979); A. Carroll (ed.), *Liberating Women's History: Theoretical and Critical Essays* (Urbana: University of Illinois

Press, 1976); J. Kelly-Gadol, "The Social Relations of the Sexes: Methodological Implications of Women's History," *Signs* 1 (1976): 809-823; J. Lewis, "Women Lost and Found: The Impact of Feminism on History," in D. Spender (ed.), *Men's Studies Modified: The Impact of Feminism on the Academic Disciplines* (Oxford and New York: Pergamon Press, 1981), pp. 73-82; and my own book *In Memory of Her: A Feminist Theological Reconstruction of Christian Origins* (New York: Crossroad, 1983), pp. 3-95.

3. Karl-Heinz Müller, "Die Haustafel des Kolosserbriefes und das antike Frauenthema: Eine kritische Rückschau auf alte Ergebnisse," in Dautzenberg, Merklein, and Müller, *Die Frau im Urchristentum*, pp. 263ff.

4. Cf. Nancy Schrom Dye, "Clio's American Daughters: Male History, Female Reality," in J. A. Sherman and E. T. Beck (eds.), *The Prism of Sex: Essays in the Sociology of Knowledge* (Madison: University of Wisconsin Press, 1979), pp. 9-31.

5. D. C. Bass, "Women's Studies and Biblical Studies: An Historical Perspective," *JSOT* 22 (1982): 6-12.

6. I. H. Marshall, "Historical Criticism," in I. Howard Marshall (ed.), *New Testament Interpretation: Essays on Principles and Methods* (Grand Rapids, Mich.: W. B. Eerdmans, 1977), pp. 126-138, p. 126.

7. Ibid., p. 127; see also E. Krentz, *The Historical-Critical Method* (Philadelphia: Fortress Press, 1975), especially pp. 33-41 with bibliography.

8. I. O. Mink, *Mind, History, and Dialectic: The Philosophy of R. G. Collingwood* (Bloomington: University of Indiana Press, 1969), pp. 162-194; and M. Earmarth, *Wilhelm Dilthey: The Critique of Historical Reason* (Chicago: University of Chicago Press, 1978), pp. 95-108.

9. The famous expression *"wie es eigentlich gewesen"* occurs in the preface, dated October 1824, to Ranke's *Geschichte der romanischen und germanischen Völker von 1494 bis 1535*. Cf. Leopold von Ranke, *The Theory and Practice of History* (eds.) G. Iggers and K. V. Moltke (Indianapolis: 1973), p. 137. The words have been translated in various ways such as "what really happened," "how it really was," or "how, essentially, things happened."

10. Cf. for example W. G. Doty, *Contemporary New Testament Interpretation* (Englewood Cliffs, N.J.: Prentice-Hall, 1972). Especially for the challenge of literary biblical criticism to historical-biblical criticism see R. A. Spencer (ed.), *Orientation by Disorientation: Studies in Literary Criticism and Biblical Literary Criticism*, Festschrift for W. A. Beardslee, Pittsburgh Theological Monograph Series 35 (Pittsburgh: Pickwick Press, 1980).

11. See for example the exchange between P. H. Nowell-Smith, "The Constructionist Theory of History," and L. J. Goldstein, "History and the Primacy of Knowing," *History and Theory: The Constitution of the Historical Past* 16 (1977): 1-52, with literature. Cf. also S. Bann, "Towards a Critical Historiography: Recent Work in the Philosophy of History," *Philosophy* 56 (1981): 365-385.

12. Cf. R. Stephen Humphreys, "The Historian, His Documents, and the Elementary Modes of Historical Thought," *History and Theory* 19 (1980): 1-20.

13. G. Leff, *History and Social Theory* (Garden City, N.Y.: Doubleday, 1971), p. 111.

14. Ibid., p. 14.

15. See the following writings by Hayden White: *Metahistory: The Historical Imagination in Nineteenth-Century Europe* (Baltimore: Johns Hopkins University Press, 1973); *Tropics of Discourse: Essays in Cultural Criticism* (Baltimore: Johns Hopkins University Press, 1978); "The Value of Narrativity in the Representation of Reality," *Critical Inquiry* 7 (1980): 5-28; "The Politics of Historical Interpretation: Discipline and De-Sublimation," in W. J. T. Mitchell (ed.), *The Politics of Interpretation* (Chicago: University of Chicago Press, 1983), pp. 119-143.

16. Hayden White, "Historicism, History, and the Figurative Imagination," *History and Theory: Essays on Historicism* 14 (1975): 54.

17. Ibid., p. 55.

18. For this influential distinction in New Testament studies see especially K. Stendahl, "Biblical Theology, Contemporary," *IDB* 1:418-432. See also chapter 6.

19. Cf. Th. Schieder, "The Role of Historical Consciousness in Political Action," *History and Theory: Historical Consciousness and Political Action* 17 (1978): pp. 3-4.

20. Dye, "Clio's American Daughters," p. 9.

21. L. Krieger, "Elements of Early Historicism: Experience, Theory, and History in Ranke," *History and Theory* 14 (1975): 8f.

22. P. Rossi, "The Ideological Valences of Twentieth-Century Historicism," *History and Theory* 14 (1975): 23.

23. W. J. Mommsen, "Social Conditioning and Social Relevance of Historical Judgments," *History and Theory* 17 (1978): 32.

24. Cf. also D. H. Porter, *The Emergence of the Past: A Theory of Historical Explanation* (Chicago: University of Chicago Press, 1981), who ends with the hope that

    if the approach to explanation outlined in this book is found useful, more and more historians will preface their narrative accounts with explanations of their theoretical and methodological presuppositions. Also philosophers of history will relate their analytic arguments more directly to actual examples of historical writing. In this way, communication can increase within a framework that grows gradually more intelligible to both sides [p.179].

25. Mommsen, "Social Conditioning," p. 33.
26. Ibid., p. 34.
27. This aspect is stressed by P. Hernadi, "Clio's Cousins: Historiography as Translation, Fiction, and Criticism," *New Literary History* 7 (1975/76): 248, who with Friedrich Schlegel argues that the historian also must always be "a prophet turned backward" who must discern in the past "what shall be remembered."
28. Cf. James Barr, "The Bible as Document of Believing Communities," in Hans Dieter Betz (ed.), *The Bible as a Document of the University* (Chico, Calif.: Scholars Press, 1981), pp. 25-47. See also chapter 2.
29. See especially F. Herzog, "Liberation Hermeneutics as Ideology Critique," *Interpretation* 27 (1974): 387-403; Juan Luis Segundo, *The Liberation of Theology* (Maryknoll, N.Y.: Orbis Books, 1976); Lee Cormie, "The Hermeneutical Privilege of the Oppressed: Liberation Theologies, Biblical Faith, and Marxist Sociology of Knowledge," *Proceedings of the Catholic Theological Society of America* 32 (1978): 155-181.
30. See chapters 1 and 3.
31. *Signs: Journal of Women in Culture and Society*, which was founded in 1975, regularly reviews feminist scholarship in various disciplines. For the most recent collections of essays on such an intellectual paradigm-shift see S. Harding and M. B. Hintikka (eds.), *Discovering Reality: Feminist Perspectives on Epistemology, Metaphysics, Methodology, and Philosophy of Science*, Synthese Library 161 (Boston: D. Reidel, 1983), and L. F. Pusch (ed.), *Feminismus: Inspektion der Herrenkultur*, Edition Suhrkamp NF 192 (Frankfurt: Suhrkamp, 1983).
32. Dorothy E. Smith, "A Sociology for Women," in Sherman and Torton Beck, *The Prism of Sex*, pp. 159f.
33. A. D. Gordon, M. J. Buhle, and N. Schrom Dye, "The Problem of Women's History," in Carroll, *Liberating Women's History*, p. 8.
34. See especially H. Smith, "Feminism and the Methodology of Women's History," in Carroll, *Liberating Women's History*, pp. 369-384; M. Zimbalist Rosaldo, "The Uses and Abuses of Anthropology: Reflections on Feminism and Cross-Cultural Understandings," *Signs* 5 (1980): 400ff; and my "Claiming the

Center: A Critical Feminist Theology of Liberation," in J. Kalven and M. I. Buckley (eds.), *Womanspirit Bonding* (New York: Pilgrim Press, 1984), pp. 292–309.

35. This classical understanding of patriarchy was developed by Aristotle and still operates in Western culture. Cf. Susan Moller Okin, *Women in Western Political Thought* (Princeton, N.J.: Princeton University Press, 1979); and chapter 4.

36. Gordon, Buhle, and Dye, "The Problem of Women's History," p. 85.

37. See my book *In Memory of Her*, especially chapters 4–8 for an attempt at such a historical reconstruction.

38. Such a procedure is not restricted to early Christian writers but is found in all forms of historiography. See P. Hernadi, "Clio's Cousins":

> The historian tends to see his [*sic*] evidence as mainly consisting of original texts. Yet all documents at his [*sic*] disposal, as well as the very work he [*sic*] is engaged in writing, are translations of the largely *nonverbal* fabric of historical events. . . . Many events, of course, have never been turned into documents and will forever escape the attention of posterity. As a result, the historian may attempt to say "nothing but the truth" but cannot expect to report "all the truth." This is a grave predicament, because as translators and other interpreters of texts know, the meaning of a whole of a text cannot be reliably construed without reference to the meaning of each part and vice versa [p.247].

39. It is obvious that I am not arguing here for the writing of historical fiction. As we have seen, historical imagination is always at work when interpreting a historical text and reconstructing a historical event. Yet in historiography historical imagination is limited and controlled by the available "evidence," while in fiction it is not. For example, it is possible to read androcentric New Testament texts as inclusive of women because on the one hand we have some clear statements that women as well as men were members of the early Christian communities, and on the other hand we have no evidence that early Christianity was an exclusively male cult. Why then do translators insist, for example, that the address "brothers" in the Pauline letters must be translated in an androcentric, exclusive way?

40. Cf. A. Rich, "Natural Resources," in *The Dream of a Common Language: Poems 1974–1977* (New York: Norton, 1978), pp. 60–67.

41. Elizabeth Fox-Genovese, "For Feminist Interpretation," *Union Seminar Quarterly Review* 35 (1979/80): 13.

172 • BREAD NOT STONE

42. Cf. Lucy S. Dawidowicz, "Lies about the Holocaust," *Commentary* 70 (1980): 31-37; cf. also her *The Holocaust and the Historians* (Cambridge, Mass.: Harvard University Press, 1981).
43. Pierre Vidal-Naquet, "A Paper Eichmann?" *Democracy* (April 1981), 93-94. For a different interpretation of Vidal-Naquet's position see Hayden White, "The Politics of Historical Interpretation," pp. 136-143. It seems to me that the issue is not "meaningfulness" or "meaninglessness" but rather historical continuity.
44. For "solidarity" as a goal of critical biblical interpretation see K. Berger, *Exegese des Neuen Testaments*, Ullstein Taschenbücher 658 (Heidelberg: Quelle and Meyer, 1977), pp. 242-269.

6. **Toward a Critical-Theological Self-Understanding of Biblical Scholarship**

1. Cf. E. Schweizer, *Luke: A Challenge to Present Theology* (Atlanta: John Knox Press, 1982), p. 56.
2. For a review and description of the historical development of biblical historical-critical scholarship, see for example R. E. Clements, *One Hundred Years of Old Testament Interpretation* (Philadelphia: Westminster Press, 1976); R. M. Grant, *A Short History of the Interpretation of the Bible*, rev. ed. (New York: Macmillan, 1963); H. F. Hahn, *The Old Testament in Modern Research*, 2nd ed. (Philadelphia: Fortress Press, 1966); P. Henry, *New Directions in New Testament Study* (Philadelphia: Westminster Press, 1979); W. G. Kümmel, *The New Testament: The History of the Investigation of Its Problems* (Nashville: Abingdon, 1972); S. Neill, *The Interpretation of the New Testament 1861-1961* (London: Oxford University Press, 1964); J. Weingreen, et al., "Interpretation, History of," *IDB* (suppl. vol.): 436-456; W. G. Doty, *Contemporary New Testament Interpretation* (Englewood Cliffs, N.J.: Prentice-Hall, 1972); Alexa Suelzer, "Modern Old Testament Criticism," in *Jerome Biblical Commentary* (Englewood Cliffs, N.J.: Prentice-Hall, 1968), vol. 2, pp. 590-604; and John S. Kselman, "Modern New Testament Criticism," in ibid., vol. 2. pp. 7-20.
3. For a spirited critique of this dichotomy in biblical studies see Walter Wink, *The Bible in Human Transformation: Toward a New Paradigm for Biblical Study* (Philadelphia: Fortress Press, 1973), and his *Transforming Bible Study: A Leader's Guide* (Nashville: Abingdon, 1980).
4. See especially Phyllis A. Bird, *The Bible as the Church's Book* (Philadelphia: Westminster Press, 1982).
5. For a review see R. Detweiler, "After the New Criticism: Contemporary Methods of Literary Interpretation," in R. A. Spencer

(ed.), *Orientation by Disorientation: Studies in Literary Criticism and Biblical Literary Criticism*, Festschrift for W. A. Beardslee, Pittsburgh Theological Monograph Series 35 (Pittburgh: Pickwick Press, 1980), pp. 3-23; N. R. Peterson, "Literary Criticism in Biblical Studies," in ibid., pp. 25-50; E. V. McKnight, "The Contours and Methods of Literary Criticism," in ibid., pp. 53-69.

6. Augustine A. Stock, "The Limits of Historical-Critical Exegesis," *BTB* 13 (1983): 28-31.
7. Leland J. White, "Historical and Literary Criticism: A Theological Reponse," *BTB* 13 (1983): 32-34.
8. Charles Davis, "The Theological Career of Historical Criticism of the Bible," *Cross Currents* 32 (1982): 267.
9. Ibid., 279.
10. See Raymond E. Brown, *Virginal Conception and Bodily Resurrection of Jesus* (New York: Paulist Press, 1973), pp. 3-11.
11. R. E. Brown, "What the Biblical Word Meant and What It Means," in his *The Critical Meaning of the Bible* (New York: Paulist Press, 1981), pp. 23-44, 36f.
12. J. Barr, "Biblical Theology," *IDB* (suppl. vol., 1976): 104-111.
13. Cf. J. D. Smart, *The Past, Present, and Future of Biblical Theology* (Philadelphia: Westminster Press, 1979).
14. B. S. Childs, *Biblical Theology in Crisis* (Philadelphia: Westminster Press, 1970), pp. 13-87, points also to the controversy on the Bible between fundamentalists and modernists that was fought between 1910 and the 1930s in American Protestantism.
15. For the following, see J. Barr, "Biblical Theology," *IDB:* 105.
16. See, for example, T. Boman, *Hebrew Thought Compared with Greek* (Philadelphia: Westminster Press, 1961); D. Hill, *Greek Words and Hebrew Meanings: Studies in the Semantics of Soteriological Terms* (Cambridge: University Press, 1967), and the review of this book by J. Barr, "Common Sense and Biblical Language," *Biblica* 49 (1968): 377-387.
17. Cf. especially J. Barr, *The Semantics of Biblical Language* (Oxford: Oxford University Press, 1961), pp. 206-219, and the review of the *status quaestionis* by A. C. Thiselton, "Semantics and New Testament Interpretation," in I. Howard Marshall (ed.), *New Testament Interpretation: Essays on Principles and Methods* (Grand Rapids, Mich.: W. B. Eerdmans, 1977), pp. 75-104.
18. See for example O. Eissfeldt, "Israelitisch-jüdische Religionsgeschichte und alttestamentliche Theologie," *ZAW* 44 (1926): 1-12. This distinction was earlier found by J. P. Gabler (1753-1826); see the discussion by H. Boers, *What is New Testament Theology?* (Philadelphia: Fortress Press, 1979), pp. 23-38.

174 • BREAD NOT STONE

19. Cf. O. Cullman, *Christ and Time: The Primitive Christian Conception of Time* (Philadelphia: Fortress Press, 1964), and *Salvation in History* (New York: Harper and Row, 1967).
20. O. Betz, "Biblical Theology, Historical," in *IDB* 1:436. For a historical review see also G. Hasel, *Old Testament Theology: Basic Issues in Current Debate*, rev. ed. (Grand Rapids, Mich.: Eerdmans, 1975), pp. 15-34.
21. For the Hebrew Bible, see J. Muilenburg, "Old Testament Scholarship: Fifty Years in Retrospect," *Journal of Bible and Religion* 28 (1960): 173-181, and G. E. Wright, "Old Testament Scholarship in Prospect," ibid.: 182-193.
22. H. J. Cadbury, "New Testament Scholarship: Fifty Years in Retrospect," *Journal of Bible and Religion* 28 (1960): 196.
23. R. M. Grant, "American New Testament Study, 1926-1956," *JBL* 87 (1968): 42.
24. Ibid., p. 50.
25. E. C. Colwell, "New Testament Scholarship in Prospect," *Journal of Bible and Religion* 28 (1960): 203.
26. See also K. Stendahl, "Method in the Study of Biblical Theology," in J. P. Hyatt (ed.), *The Bible in Modern Scholarship* (Nashville: Abingdon, 1965), pp. 196-209.
27. For differing methods in biblical theology see for example G. F. Hasel, "Methodology as a Major Problem in the Current Crisis of Old Testament Theology," *BTB* 2 (1972): 177-198. Difficulties in methodology seem to be rooted in different conceptualizations of what biblical theology should be. Cf. Boers. *What Is New Testament Theology?*, for such a perspective.
28. K. Stendahl, "Biblical Theology, Contemporary," *IDB* 1:422.
29. Ibid., p. 424.
30. Ibid., p. 431.
31. Stendahl, "Method in the Study of Biblical Theology," p. 199.
32. Boers, *What Is New Testament Theology?*, p. 85.
33. A. Dulles, S.J., "Response to Krister Stendahl's 'Method in the Study of Biblical Theology,'" in Hyatt, *The Bible in Modern Scholarship*, pp. 210-211.
34. R. de Vaux, "Method in the Study of Early Hebrew History," in *The Bible in Modern Scholarship* pp. 15f. Cf. G. E. Mendenhall's criticism of R. de Vaux's proposal and the traditional division of academic labor, ibid., pp. 30f.
35. The trenchant critique of historical criticism does not so much pertain to its methods but to its rationalist and agnostic presuppositions. Among others see Peter Stuhlmacher, *Historical Criticism and Theological Interpretation of Scripture: Toward a Hermeneutics of Consent* (Philadelphia: Fortress Press, 1977); D. C.

Steinmetz, "The Superiority of Pre-Critical Exegesis," *Theology Today* 37 (1980): 27-37.

36. Cf. for example O. Kaiser and W. G. Kümmel, *Exegetical Method: A Student's Handbook*, rev. ed. (New York: Seabury, 1981); R. N. Soulen, *Handbook of Biblical Criticism* (Atlanta: John Knox Press, 1976); D. J. Harrington, *Interpreting the New Testament: A Practical Guide* (Wilmington: M. Glazier, 1979); E. Krentz, *The Historical-Critical Method* (Philadelphia: Fortress Press, 1975); J. H. Hayes and C. R. Holladay, *Biblical Exegesis: A Beginner's Handbook* (Atlanta: John Knox Press, 1982); K. Berger, *Exegese des Neuen Testaments*, Ullstein Taschenbücher 658 (Heidelberg: Quelle and Meyer, 1977); and the popular account of J. J. Collins, "Methods and Presuppositions of Biblical Scholarship," *Chicago Studies* (Spring 1978): 5-28.

37. Cf. for example W. A. Beardslee, *Literary Criticism of the New Testament* (Philadelphia: Fortress Press, 1970); D. Patte, *What Is Structural Exegesis?* (Philadephia: Fortress Press, 1976).

38. For a discussion and review of the "social world" study see the contributions in *Interpretation* 37 (1982): 229-277.

39. See for example R. Polzin, *Biblical Structuralism* (Missoula, Mon.: Scholars Press, 1977): I. Soter, "The Dilemma of Literary Science," *New Literary History* 2 (1970): 85-100.

40. P. Hernadi, "Literary Theory: A Compass for Critics," *Critical Inquiry* 3 (1976/77): 369-386, 369.

41. L. E. Keck, "Will the Historical-Critical Method Survive? Some Observations," in R. A. Spencer (ed.), *Orientation by Disorientation*, p. 124.

42. See for example Schweizer, *Luke: A Challenge to Present Theology*, p. 12: "Historico-critical methods are certainly not necessary for the salvation of the individual believer. But if we prohibited them or limited their functions anxiously, we would forget that God became incarnate in the earthly history of a human being, called Jesus of Nazareth. If on the other hand, we thought that historico-critical research were just everything and the only basis of faith, we could forget it was God who became flesh in this history,"

43. Cf. R. E. Brown, "Hermeneutics," *JBC* II (1968): 605-623; R. E. Palmer, *Hermeneutics* (Evanston, Ill.: Northwestern University Press, 1969); R. Lapointe, "Hermeneutics Today," *BTB* 2 (1972): 107-154; and A. C. Thiselton, *The Two Horizons: New Testament Hermeneutics and Philosophical Descriptions with Special Reference to Heidegger, Bultmann, Gadamer, and Wittgenstein* (Grand Rapids, Mich.: Eerdmans, 1980), for review of the problems and literature.

176 • BREAD NOT STONE

44. Cf. P. Ricoeur, *Interpretation Theory: Discourse and Surplus of Meaning* (Forth Worth, Tex.: Christian University Press, 1976), and *Essays on Biblical Interpretation* (Philadelphia: Fortress Press, 1980); and J. W. Van den Hengel, *The Home of Meaning: The Hermeneutics of the Subject of Paul Ricoeur* (Washington, D.C.: University of America Press, 1983), pp. 192ff.
45. Cf. G. N. Stanton, "Presuppositions in New Testament Criticism," in Marshall, *New Testament Interpretation*, pp. 60-71.
46. Cf. his "Is Exegesis without Presuppositions Possible?" in S. M. Ogden (ed.), *Existence and Faith* (London: Hodder and Stoughton, 1961), pp. 342-251.
47. For the following discussion cf. A. C. Thiselton, "The New Hermeneutic," in Marshall, *New Testament Interpretation*, pp. 308-333.
48. Cf. T. Peters, "The Nature and Role of Presuppositions: An Inquiry into Contemporary Hermeneutics," *International Philosophical Quarterly* 14 (1974): 209-222.
49. P. Stuhlmacher, *Historical Criticism and Theological Interpretation of Scripture*, p. 90.
50. Thiselton, "The New Hermeneutic," p. 310.
51. Sandra M. Schneiders, "Faith, Hermeneutics, and the Literal Sense of Scripture," *Theological Studies* 39 (1978): 733.
52. Ibid., p. 735.
53. Ibid., p. 733.
54. Cf. for example E. Cardenal (ed.), *The Gospel in Solentiname*, 2 vols. (Maryknoll, N.Y.: Orbis books, 1976), vol. 1, p. vii: "the commentaries of the *campesinos* are usually of greater profundity than that of many theologians."
55. For a concrete example of how such a critical evaluative hermeneutic proceeds, see chapter 4.
56. P. D. Hanson, "The Responsibility of Biblical Theology to Communities of Faith," *Theology Today* 37 (1980): 40.
57. A. Schlatter, "Atheistische Methoden in der Theologie," in *Zur Theologie des Neuen Testaments und zur Dogmatik*, Theologische Bücherei 41 (Munich: Chr. Kaiser Verlag, 1969), pp. 138f.
58. See my "Feminist Theology as a Critical Theology of Liberation" *Theological Studies* 36 (1975): 605-626; "Toward a Liberating and Liberated Theology: Women Theologians and Feminist Theology in the U.S.A.," *Concilium* 115 (1979): 22-32; and "Claiming the Center: A Critical Feminist Theology of Liberation," in M. I. Buckley and J. Kalven (eds.), *Womanspirit Bonding* (New York: Pilgrim Press, 1984), pp. 292-309.
59. Cf. for example J. H. Cone, "Christian Faith and Political Praxis," in Brian Mahan and L. Dale Richesin (eds.), *The Chal-*

lenge of Liberation Theology: A First World Response (Maryknoll, N.Y.: Orbis Press, 1981), pp. 60–61: "If faith is the belief that God created all for freedom, then praxis is the social theory used to analyze the structures of injustice so that we will know what must be done for the historical realization of freedom. To sing about freedom and to pray for its coming is not enough. Freedom must be actualized in history by oppressed peoples who accept the intellectual challenge to analyze the world for the purpose of changing it. . . . The truth of the gospel then is a truth that must be done and not simply spoken. To speak the truth without doing the truth is to contradict the truth one claims to affirm."

60. J. E. Weir, "The Bible and Marx: A Discussion of the Hermeneutics of Liberation Theology," *Scot. Journal of Theology* 35 (1982): 344. Cf. also J. A. Kirk, "The Bible in Latin American Liberation Theology," in N. Cottwald and A. Wire (eds.), *The Bible and Liberation* (Berkeley, Calif.: Radical Religion Reader, 1976), pp. 157–165.

61. See especially Lee Cormie, "The Hermeneutical Privilege of the Oppressed: Liberation Theologies, Biblical Faith, and Marxist Sociology of Knowledge," *Proceedings of the Catholic Theological Society of America* 32 (1977): 155–181.

62. See for example Schubert M. Ogden, *Faith and Freedom: Toward a Theology of Liberation* (Nashville: Abingdon, 1979), and my critique of his objections in chapter 3.

63. See my *In Memory of Her: A Feminist Theological Reconstruction of Christian Origins* (New York: Crossroad, 1983), p. 41–96.

64. Cf. F. Herzog, "Liberation Hermeneutics as Ideology Critique," *Interpretation* 27 (1974): 387–403; D. Lockhead, "Hermeneutics and Ideology," *Ecumenist* 15 (1977): 81–84.

65. See Juan Luis Segundo, *The Liberation of Theology* (Maryknoll, N.Y.: Orbis Books, 1976), pp. 8f. See also the evaluation of Segundo's work by A. Hennelly, *Theologies in Conflict: The Challenge of Juan Luis Segundo* (Maryknoll, N.Y.: Orbis Books, 1979); A. J. Tambasco, *The Bible for Ethics: Juan Luis Segundo and First World Ethics* (Washington, D.C.: University of America Press, 1981).

66. Cf. for example, E. Tamez, *Bible of the Oppressed* (Maryknoll, N.Y.: Orbis Books, 1982), who has very little to say about women.

67. This was underlined by both B. Birch's and T. Ogletree's response to my "Discipleship and Patriarchy," pp. 173–189.

68. For a different position emphasizing the prophetic traditions in the Bible as such a liberating tradition and principle see Rose-

mary Radford Ruether, "The Feminist Critique in Religious Studies," *Soundings* 64 (1981): 388-402, and "Feminism and Patriarchal Religion: Principles of Ideological Critique of the Bible," *JSOT* 22 (1982): 54-66.

69. Segundo, *The Liberation of Theology*, p. 179.

70. J. Donovan, "Feminism and Aesthetics," *Critical Inquiry* 3 (1976/77): 608, and *Feminist Literary Criticism: Explorations in Theory* (Lexington: University Press of Kentucky, 1975), who argues for a "prescriptive" criticism or a criticism that exists "in the prophetic mode," compared to a "purely aesthetic criticism and judgment" of literature.

71. James Barr, "The Bible as a Document of Believing Communities," in Hans Dieter Betz (ed.), *The Bible as a Document of the University* (Chico, Calif.: Scholars Press, 1981), p. 38.

72. This seems to me the most of what one can say about the "overall theological coherence" of the canon. See the review by B. W. Anderson of B. S. Childs, *Introduction to the Old Testament as Scripture* in *Theology Today* 37 (1980): 100-108; for a contrasting evaluation of B. S. Childs and J. Sanders see E. E. Lemcio, "The Gospels and Canonical Criticism," *BTB* 11 (1981): 114-122, and J. Sanders' response, pp. 122-124. For an integration of "canonical" criticism into liberation theology see L. J. White, "Biblical Theologians and Theologies of Liberation: Part I, Canon-Supporting Framework," *BTB* 11 (1981): 35-40, and "Part II, Midrash Applies Text to Context," ibid.: 98-103.

73. *RSR* 7 (1981): 283.

74. See chapter 3 and the responses by A. C. Wire, B. Birch, B. Gaventa, and D. Setel at the AAR panel sponsored by Feminist Hermeneutic Project and Liberation Theology Group at the AAR annual meeting in New York in 1982.

75. See for example S. Bann, "Towards a Critical Historiography: Recent Work in Philosophy of History," *Philosophy* 56 (1981): 365-385, and the exchange between P. H. Nowell-Smith, "The Constructionist Theory of History," and L. J. Goldstein, "History and the Primacy of Knowing," *History and Theory* 16 (1977): 1-52.

76. Cf. G. Leff, *History and Social Theory* (Garden City, N.Y.: Doubleday, 1971); R. Stephen Humphreys. "The Historian, His Documents, and the Elementary Modes of Historical Thought," *History and Theory* 19 (1980): 1-20.

77. Cf. especially the writings of Hayden White: "The Value of Narrativity in the Representation of Reality," *Critical Inquiry* 7 (1980): 5-28; "Historicism, History, and the Figurative Imagina-

tion," *History and Theory* 14 (1975): 43-67; "The Politics of Historical Interpretation: Discipline and De-Sublimation," in W. J. T. Mitchell (ed.), *The Politics of Interpretation* (Chicago: University of Chicago Press, 1983), pp. 119-143.

78. Cf. Nancy Schrom Dye, "Clio's American Daughters: Male History, Female Reality," in J. A. Sherman and E. Torton Beck (eds.), *The Prism of Sex: Essays in the Sociology of Knowledge* (Madison: University of Wisconsin Press, 1979), pp. 9-31.

79. See also the Inaugural Address of W. Sibley Towner, "Enlisting Exegesis in the Cause of the Church," who shared with me an unpublished copy at the workshop in Villanova. Cf. also E. C. Ulrich and W. G. Thompson, "The Tradition as a Resource in Theological Reflection: Scripture and the Minister," in J. Whitehead and E. Eaton Whitehead (eds.), *Method in Ministry: Theological Reflection and Christian Ministry* (New York: Seabury, 1980), pp. 31-52.

80. Cf. also E. W. Said, "Opponents, Audiences, Constituencies, and Community," in Mitchell, *The Politics of Interpretation*, pp. 7-32.

81. G. Shaw, *The Cost of Authority: Manipulation and Freedom in the New Testament* (Philadelphia: Fortress Press, 1983), p. 275. Although there are many problems with its exegetical readings, the book's hermeneutic points toward biblical scholarship for Christian liberation praxis.

82. W. C. Booth, "Freedom of Interpretation: Bakhtin and the Challenge of Feminist Criticism," in Mitchell, *The Politics of Interpretation*, pp. 51-82.

83. Cf. also G. Strecker, " 'Biblische Theologie'? Kritische Bemerkungen zu den Entwürfen von Hartmut Gese und Peter Stuhlmacher," in D. Lührmann and G. Strecker (eds.), *Kirche, Festschrift für Günther Bornkamm zum 75. Geburtstag* (Tübingen: JCB Mohr, 1980), pp. 425-445, 443f, who argues for a more critical clarification of the presuppositions of the interpretive process than a hermeneutics of consent can allow for.

84. Cf. for example R. R. Gillogly, "Spanking Hurts Everybody," *Theology Today* 37 (1980): 415-424; S. Brooks Thistlethwaite, "Battered Woman and the Bible: From Subjection to Liberation," *Christianity and Crisis* 41 (1981): 303-313. Cf. The review of interpretations by Willard Swartley, *Slavery, Sabbath, War, and Women: Case Studies in Biblical Interpretation* (Philadelphia: Herald Press, 1983), who argues for the Bible as "resource" and "guide" but does not sufficiently take into account the violence perpetuated by biblical texts.

85. P. Hernadi, "Clio's Cousins: Historiography as Translation, Fiction, and Criticism," *New Literary History* 7 (1975/76): 247-257.
86. Ibid., p. 250.
87. This is also recognized by F. Hahn, "Probleme historischer Kritik," *ZNTW* 63 (1972): 14-17.
88. For the literature and discussion see my *In Memory of Her*, pp. 68-95.
89. J. A. Sanders, "Hermeneutics," *IDB* (suppl. vol.): 407.
90. Barr, "The Bible as Document of Believing Communities," p. 39.
91. W. J. Mommsen, "Social Conditioning and Social Relevance of Historical Judgments," *History and Theory* 17 (1978): 32f.
92. Cf. also the excellent contribution of Francis Schüssler Fiorenza, "Critical Social Theology and Christology: Toward an Understanding of Atonement and Redemption as Emancipatory Solidarity," *Proceedings of the Catholic Theological Society of America* 30 (1975): 63-100. For "solidarity" as the goal of biblical interpretation see K. Berger, *Exegese des Neuen Testaments*, pp. 242-269.

Index